Life Wide Open

One Girl's Extraordinary Journey

SHERYN ADAMSON

WESTBOW
P R E S S®
A DIVISION OF THOMAS NELSON
& ZONDERVAN

WestBow Press books may be ordered through booksellers or by contacting:

WestBow Press
A Division of Thomas Nelson & Zondervan
1663 Liberty Drive
Bloomington, IN 47403
www.westbowpress.com
1 (866) 928-1240

ISBN: 978-1-9736-1279-7 (sc)
ISBN: 978-1-9736-1280-3 (hc)
ISBN: 978-1-9736-1278-0 (e)

Library of Congress Control Number: 2017919757

Print information available on the last page.

WestBow Press rev. date: 1/23/2018

This book is dedicated to ...

My husband Brad and two beautiful girls, Tayla and Rylee.

My girls: compassionate yet passionate. Kind yet fierce. Gentle yet strong-hearted. Your beauty within and without takes my breath away. Your faith in God, so pure. You make me laugh, you challenge me, you encourage me. I have so much fun with you! I thank God that he would allow Dad and me to be your parents. This is a priceless gift God has given us. You were both totally worth the long, hard and painful wait. Good things take time, I guess! I love you both so fiercely, my daughters. Stay close to Jesus and chase your dreams.

My husband Bradley John: I've told you before, but I could not have picked a better, more perfect person to marry. Your strong and protective love for me and our girls is unchallenged. Your support and encouragement for me during this book-writing process has been unwavering, and I thank you for that. For the memories we are creating on this adventure we are doing together – I love it! I honour you as an amazing godly father and husband. I love you, my precious best friend.

RECOMMENDATIONS ...

Sheryn is a marvellous writer — totally honest and candid, yet discreet, and a natural storyteller. And so funny! Delightful, moving, thought-provoking stuff. She has another great gift — the ability to talk about Christianity without being off putting. Her book is different. Her decency and spirit shine through, as does the quality and wit of her storytelling. She deserves a wide audience — so many people could benefit so much from this story.
Roger Steele, Publisher.

****

Sheryn unlocks her heart and invites us inside as she recounts her journey with God. This book offers a buffet of emotion: joy, grief, regret, laughter, conviction, hope and blessing—all presented in one powerful experience. Sheryn's style is conversational and the vulnerability she displays gives me permission to be vulnerable as a reader. This book is God-breathed and I believe carries an invitation for the Holy Spirit to bring healing and wholeness to any willing heart.
Shar Davis, Salvation Army.

****

It takes a peculiar kind of courage and stamina to write one's own story. Sheryn Adamson is a courageous woman, telling not just the facts of her growing years, her life as a policewoman, and then as a mother and style consultant, but also her inner journey through vulnerability, loss, and being shaped by the relentless, amazing grace of God.
Barbara Sampson, Author.

****

I've never wanted to be a police officer, I didn't meet my husband the first day on the job, I've never faced down infertility or run a marathon (not a literal one, anyway), I wouldn't know the first thing about my 'style personality' and I've never had to bury guinea pigs. And yet I met myself again and again in Sheryn's wonderful story. In this Facebook-world of carefully curated selfies and posts, here is a woman who totally tells it like it is. A story of finding love and living with hope amidst the unanswered questions of life. 'Life Wide Open', indeed!
Christina Tyson, Editor.

Acknowledgements

Acknowledgements: The recognition of the importance or quality of something. And so, this must include ...

My Heavenly Father, the ultimate beautiful creator, God. I thank you for my life you have created. Without you, no me. I can say the same to my parents. *Without you, no me.* I thank you for the most amazing, godly, good, genuine, humble, kind and loving people that you are. Parents, friends, mentors and brilliant grandparents. Craig and I are blessed to be your children.

Craig. My number-one brother! The history and memories we share as brother and sister are incomparable. What a journey we have had and do have together. Your tender-heartedness is beautiful and inspires me. Also, such a gifted musician, I admire and love you deeply.

To Kaye and Warner, brother and sisters-in-law. Thank you for sharing your lives, son and brother with me. I am grateful for the love we share as family and the adventures we have had and will continue to have together.

To other family members, dear friends and work colleagues. Again, without you all there is no book. There are no stories to tell. You, in many different ways, have made my life so full. So fun. To be able to share some huge highs and have you help me through my lows — for all that, I am so grateful.

And then, of course, those special people who turned my sometimes rambling words into a book I believe is worth reading ...

Major Christina Tyson, editor extraordinaire. The hours you have spent on this manuscript — invaluable. For your laughter, your honesty, your guidance, understanding and expertise, I am truly grateful.

Salvation Army officers Majors Barbara Sampson, Judith Bennett and Shar Davis, along with Roger Steele, Mandy Carian, Vivienne Hill, Ingrid Barratt and Mum —thanks to all of you for giving your time to read my manuscript along its long and evolving journey. For your comments, suggestions, guidance, collective wisdom, and picking up things even Spellcheck has no idea about ... thank you so much!

Finally, to my dear friend Sergeant Jamie Bradley who went to Heaven on the 7th of July 2017. In October of 2016, not knowing I was writing a book and not knowing how discouraged I was feeling that month, you rang and said, 'Sheryn, I think I have a message from God for you. I can't get these words out of my head and your name keeps coming to mind with these words. The words for you Sheryn are: *God has set you a task to complete.*' Complete it I have, Jamie. Thank you.

Contents

Author's Note

I see this book as the record of a journey. The journey of a girl doing life the best she can on this earth. Shaped and influenced by events along her way.

Throughout my life I've journaled. I've kept diaries — not religiously, but at different and usually significant stages — writing down thoughts, memories and ideas simply for myself.

Then, around the age of 30, I wrote what seemed at the time to be a random chapter of a then unwritten book. It was about an incident I dealt with as a police officer, an event that scarred me. It helped to get this out of my head and onto paper.

Sometime later I penned another few chapters for this non-existent book, this time about a dark personal time as I faced down infertility. Again, I filed these pages away.

A decade on, now in my mid-forties, I came across all these pages again. An idea formed and I thought: *Maybe, just maybe, all these thoughts, memories and 'chapters' written over the years could be shared and possibly encourage someone else on their journey.*

My writing is honest. In places it is very personal, sometimes raw — and in sharing these parts of myself I feel incredibly vulnerable. Yet, when I've had time to sit down and write, literally with pen and paper, the words have flowed easily, like they were meant to be. A memoir, I guess, has emerged.

By nature I'm a quiet person. An introvert, relishing and preferring time alone. But, when with people — and because of my life's experiences and opportunities — I have learnt and taught myself to be pretty good at giving off extroverted qualities. And I do genuinely love people.

I'm happy and confident enough to speak in front of hundreds, so long as I'm passionate about my topic. I like to be with people. However, given the chance, being at home or somewhere by myself where I don't have to speak, but can instead just be, read, potter or people watch? Bliss.

Once, at a wedding, I was chatting to a friend about some of the journey my husband and I had been on and my friend made the comment, 'You know, you really should write a book sometime.' *Interesting*, I thought to myself.

Some months later, I sent an email to a group of girlfriends about an event I had just gone through, and a couple of them made the comment, 'You really should write a book.' My thoughts were being confirmed and the desire was growing as I knew I already had a few chapters tucked away.

I enjoy running. Well, most of the time. While I run I do lots of thinking. I work through issues I'm facing. I plan, pray and think. I was doing this one day, forming another 'chapter' in my mind, when a voice said, 'You should write that down.' I laughed (not out loud — I didn't want to look like a mad woman) and thought: *You already know I'm writing these things down.*

Now, some of you have probably just questioned: *What is this woman on about? She hears 'voices' in her head and talks back to them?* Well, yes I do sometimes, and I'll talk more about that later. So hold that thought.

My challenge is, don't judge me yet on what I've just said.

Read my book, cover to cover, and then if you still think I'm a bit crazy, at least you will be making an informed judgment.

As I share my life with you, I hope you realise that, really, we are all very similar. We all enter life the same way and finish the same way, to a greater or lesser degree. Things that happen on our journey shape and mould us. Experiences influence the paths we take, our beliefs, passions, behaviour and decisions. We can all be scarred by events in life. We all have secrets and carry burdens.

But I believe life is a journey with a purpose and a plan. I don't believe it is just a set of random events.

Do I mention God, Jesus, Heaven, in this book? Yes I do, unashamedly so. But however you have come to be reading my book right now, I challenge you to finish it. *Do you have to believe in God? Absolutely not!* I still hope you might laugh and cry your way through this journey with me. I hope my words provoke you. Maybe you judge yourself and others a little less harshly because of what you read here. I hope you will be encouraged. I hope that along the way you may be intrigued about this God I keep referring to. Or not. Perfectly fine too. *Truly!*

At the start of January 2015, I turned on the TV one evening and an advert for Jeep vehicles was playing. The well-spoken man doing the voiceover was saying, 'Right now you are writing the story of your life — the question is: would anyone want to read it?'

'Well, I hope so,' I said out loud to the TV man!

So, indulge me as I invite you to come on this very open and raw journey. Experience through my eyes what has happened along the way and shaped me into the person I am today.

— *Sheryn Adamson*

Take your everyday, ordinary life—your sleeping, eating, going-to-work, and walking-around life—and place it before God as an offering. Embracing what God does for you is the best thing you can do for him. ... You'll be changed from the inside out. ... God brings the best out of you, develops well-formed maturity in you.

— Romans 12:1-2 (MSG)

Setting The Scene

In the beginning there is a girl. Merilyn Probert. The beautiful eldest daughter of an Air New Zealand pilot. Her parents live in Wellington, New Zealand's capital. They have five other children. Tragically, her youngest brother dies at fourteen months. He had a number of physical deformities, but ultimately passed away of double pneumonia. Family life isn't devoid of hardships, but it's happy and loving.

Mel has an endearing nature. She does well at school, plays sport, and has singing, speech, ballet, swimming and piano lessons. She makes her decisions from the heart more than the head.

And there is a doctor. He and his wife have a daughter and a son, Garth McKenzie. They too have made the stunning harbour city of Wellington their home. Theirs is also a happy family upbringing. They too experience trauma. The boy's beautiful mother dies at fifty-three of a brain tumour, when he is just twenty-one.

The father, the doctor, remarries. Life continues. The boy sees life in black and white, right and wrong, and is very organised. His decisions are made from the head more than the heart. He plays sport, rugby and cricket, and has a passion for yachting, competing on Wellington's harbour.

The doctor pays home visits to the pilot's family many times, as one did in the 'olden days'. The doctor has noticed the pilot's eldest daughter and thinks his son might approve of this young lady.

The son and daughter meet. He and she do approve of each other. Very much. They start courting — again, something that happened in the olden days. The pilot's daughter and the doctor's son fall in love, and in time he proposes. She says yes! Their journey together begins.

My parents married in 1968. Garth was, at the time, working as Personnel Manager at the hugely popular fashion store James Smiths, Wellington. Mel was employed as Private Secretary to an accountant at the Dominion Life insurance company.

A little house in a suburb called Ngaio was purchased. In 1971, their first-born daughter arrived. My journey began. Life was happy and sweet.

One day, however, while my father was in his office at James Smiths, alone, he heard a voice. An audible voice. The voice said, 'Be an officer for me.' If my father writes a book, which I am encouraging my parents to do, I'm sure this will be a part of his story.

So, yes, the hearing voices thing runs in our family — but for me, not audibly.

What that audible voice meant to my dad was that he believed God was speaking to him. God was asking him to leave his current job and to become a full-time minister — an officer, pastor — in The Salvation Army church.

This meant my parents would need to leave their full-time paid jobs, sell their home, and package up life as they knew it to move and live at The Salvation Army Training College. They did.

At its best, being a Salvation Army officer is a giving, selfless and serving job. Mum and Dad sacrificed their ambitions to train for the next two years to become officers in The Salvation Army.

So began a different journey. In 1973 we moved to where the Training College was based at the time – Aro Valley, Wellington. (I'll actually bring you back here with me in chapter eight, some twenty years later.) Along with twenty-four other people, training began. Not for me, I was only two years old.

During the next two years my brother Craig was conceived. Scandal! *No, no, no to conceiving babies while in training — oh well, what can you do?*

1974. We are in New Plymouth, on what is called 'out training'. Getting some on-the-job experience. It is here my little brother was born; our family was now complete. We left as three, but return to Wellington as a family of four, so Mum and Dad can finish their training.

Mum and Dad are 'commissioned' as officers and receive their first rank as Salvation Army lieutenants in 1975.

This basically means they passed all the tests — apart from failing the one about not making babies while in training! (I was pretty pleased about that as I got a little brother out of the scandal.) They learnt how to preach sermons from the bible, lead songs, conduct weddings and funerals, counsel people and basically run a church.

They are let loose to serve God with the gifts they have and the tools they have been taught. That means my brother and I are along for the ride, not much of a choice to be had at the ages of zero and three.

First stop, 1975, Taupo. The central part of New Zealand's North Island. Situated beside the shores of the beautiful Lake Taupo. Mountains Ruapehu, Ngarahoe and Tongariro all visible from the lake in summer. Stunningly snow-capped and perfect for skiing in the middle of winter.

School number one for me: Tongariro Primary School. My one and only clear memory is of getting lost during a combined school athletics day.

This wee five-year-old obviously missed the memo about sticking with the group of bigger kids she was assigned to and/or the teachers thought young Sheryn would know where to go. Not so. Somehow I was 'lost' but also found within the safety of the school grounds. I was so traumatised Mum had to come and take me home.

We spend two years in Taupo, then we are off to Greymouth. Just over 800 km south, situated on the West Coast of the picturesque South Island. This allows us as a family to explore parts of New Zealand we may not otherwise have seen.

Greymouth Primary School — hours of fun on the monkey bars! Visiting nearby Shanty Town, a recreated gold mining town. I don't remember Greymouth always being wet, despite what people often say about the West Coast. I do remember our cat giving birth to a litter of kittens.

My brother and I decide the kittens would look good in Mum's china cabinet. Helping put said kittens into the cabinet, and in my rush to keep them contained, I close the door a little too quickly on the last kitten. This causes much pain for the poor little feline. The kitten's tail, when released, is literally hanging by a white thread. I can vividly see that to this day.

Dad, being the son of a doctor, was asked (well, ordered amidst the angst of screaming children) to 'fix' the tail. Doctor's son did so with a pair of scissors.

Snip. Done. Tail gone. The kitten lives and enjoys a happy, if tail-less, life at the home of one of the kind people from our Greymouth Salvation Army church.

1978. We move further south to Christchurch, in the Canterbury region. Settle into the suburb of St Albans for the next four years, and I enjoy Paparoa Street Primary School. Fond memories of Dad being on pool-cleaning duties at our school pool. This means a key to the school pool. Perfect for hot Canterbury summer days.

My father's posting for The Salvation Army in Christchurch was Divisional Youth and Candidates Secretary. Mum was not given a specific role, but shared responsibilities in organising camps. Craig and I got to attend many of these camps, well before we were of eligible age. Fun! These times shaped my sense of being safe and secure in my family and my love of all things adventurous and outdoors.

Camps were fun with your parents at that age. It was their job to help kids enjoy themselves — a blessing I treasure. This time helped make me a confident, secure person. Both Mum and Dad on hand to help, guide, love and direct if need be. Mine were 'present' parents, which I know is not always the norm — and I am so grateful.

My relationship with my brother Craig grew strong during this time. We have always been (and are still) very close. Despite all the moving around, we always had each other. We are similar in so many ways, yet also very different.

I treasure our precious relationship. Thinking back, I know this bond is what made our lifestyle of moving around so much, more manageable.

But then, after four years in the South, the phone call comes that we are on the move again. (Such phone calls usually came before we left for school.)

Let me explain about the 'phone call' ...

Don't be afraid to change. You may lose something good but you may gain something better.

— Anon

The Phone Call

Every year in November, on a given date, Salvation Army officers all around New Zealand would hover around their landline phones. (Attached to the wall or curly-cord phones — no hands-free or cell phones.) A call would come in from Salvation Army Headquarters in Wellington, from those 'higher up' (where the bosses hang out) who had the duty, privilege and power to move officers to different appointments within New Zealand, and worldwide if needed.

Think of people in the military or navy or other corporations. As part of signing up for the job, you know at some point your boss has the power to move you and your family to wherever, whenever they feel it necessary. This is how it is for Salvation Army officers, too.

As I got older I would sense anxiety leading up to the 'phone call' when my parents had a 'feeling' that a move was on the cards. Or I would also sense the peace when they thought the phone call would be short and sweet, because it was a 'no move this year' call.

It's 2015 as I write this chapter. If you have any love of rugby and/or knowledge of the All Blacks, you will understand the significance of this year. The thirty-one members of the

All Blacks Squad for the Rugby World Cup have just been announced. Much was made in the media about those All Blacks on the fringe of selection. How hard it must have been for them waiting on that Sunday morning phone call.

Waiting is hard. Was the call that was coming positive or negative? Was it life-changing, Rugby World Cup 2015 adventure? Or was it devastation and the heartbreaking words, 'Sorry, you've not been picked'?

I understand their anxiety! It's very hard when your future is in the hands of another. One simple phone call and life, from that day forward, can take you on the journey you hope for. Or your life takes a different path, disappointment perhaps leading the way.

The call came for our family. Four years after living happily in Christchurch our time was up in the South Island and we were on the move to the North Island. Again.

A long journey, we found out, moving from Christchurch to Auckland. One cream Cortina station wagon with no air-conditioning — pre iPods, iPads, DVDs and computer games. Two adults, two children and one unhappy cat, this one with its tail attached. A ferry ride between the South and North Island to break up the journey. A long hot couple of days travelling in summer from the south to the north.

Destination: Auckland. More new schools. Last year of primary school for me.

I join and enjoy being part of a running team. Running is still one of my favourite 'time-out' activities. As I've already said, it's when I do lots more than just run. My mind is also very busy.

In Auckland, I experience my one and only detention. It's the one day Dad says, 'Don't be late after school, Sheryn; we will be waiting outside in the car to go to an appointment.' I am late. I had to pick up rubbish after school as a punishment.

Mum comes in to find out why I was taking so long. I tell

her I've decided to help pick up rubbish after school that day. Trying to talk my way out of a situation I was embarrassed about. (I didn't like being in trouble, doing something wrong, and I didn't like being late for things. Still don't, for both things.)

I am bell monitor at school. *Power, I love it!* (Yeah, I still like being in charge.)

During my last year at primary school a friend, whose mother had the key for the school canteen, and I manage to sneak that key one lunchtime when the canteen is closed.

We enjoy our own personal shopping spree in that little room, filling empty biscuit boxes with treasures and treats. Then, with our loot, we scamper, hiding behind the caretaker's shed to eat ourselves sick. Chippies, chocolate and lollies. (First and only attempt, I must add, at shoplifting. I shake my head now in disbelief at that young girl! What was I thinking?)

My first year at Intermediate. Avondale Intermediate.

First time bussing to school by myself. First time seeing school kids smoke and being offered cigarettes. Feeling peer pressure, but willing to stand up for what I did or did not want to do. First (and only) time seeing my school classroom and everything in it burn to the ground after being targeted by arsonists.

Seeing my male teacher in tears at losing all the resources he'd built up over years and years of being a teacher. Gone. I didn't feel sad for me and what I had lost; I felt sad, angry and a huge sense of injustice for my teacher. I felt helpless for him.

All these seemingly insignificant things that happened to me were moulding me. What I experienced, saw, dealt with — all of them shaping me into the person I am today. I'm amazed at how much like a jigsaw, starting with one piece at a time to create the full, detailed picture, life is.

1984. Phone call day. The call doesn't come before Craig and I leave for school. Which is unusual. Lunchtime (again, remember, no cell phones), I march confidently into the school office and explain that I need to use the phone to call home, please. A conversation unfolds with the office lady …

'Are you unwell?'

'No, I need to see if me and my family are moving or not.'

'Has your house been on the market?'

'No, we don't own our house, The Salvation Army does. But today we get told by Mum and Dad's boss if they want us to move from Auckland or if we get to stay for another year.'

'Oh.'

Phone call home is made.

'Hi Sheryn. Yes we are moving; we are going to Palmerston North.'

'Oh.' My hand goes over the receiver, then addressing the office lady, 'Where is Palmerston North?'

No reply from confused office lady. I ask her, 'Do you have a map?' Still no reply.

'Sheryn, we'll talk about it when you and Craig get home and we'll explain where Palmerston North is. Okay?'

'Okay.'

Thank you to office lady. Bemused smile in return.

Back to class wondering what my sixth school would be like? Wondering where Palmerston North is — big, small, North Island, or back to the South? (I wish we'd had Google back then.)

We find Palmerston North. Mum and Dad seem to know where to go without Google maps or GPS. Impressive. It's quite a bit smaller than Auckland, we discover. Quite a few hours south of Auckland, we discover, as does our unhappily caged cat.

Remember to celebrate milestones as you prepare for the road ahead.

— Nelson Mandela

Milestones

Five great years, two schools and lots of good friends made in Palmerston North.

Despite being shy and quiet by nature, I'd become practised at being bold. Feeling the fear, but doing it anyway, and walking up to kids to involve myself in their groups.

Often teachers, in my younger years, would say, 'This is Sheryn, she is the new girl, who can look after her?' But as I got older, teachers didn't do that so much. It was more a case of fend for yourself. So I did.

My first day at Intermediate Normal School in Palmerston North. I don't know a soul. I have spent morning tea by myself, which is kind of okay for an introvert, but I know school is better with friends. I mentally prepare myself for doing something about this at lunchtime.

When the bell rings announcing it is time for Sheryn to be brave and make friends, I get my lunch and stand back, watching. I spy a group of three or four girls sitting on the ground starting their lunch. I make them my target. I walk over and confidently ask, 'Can I have lunch with you please?'

With butterflies causing havoc inside my stomach — and

not because I was hungry — I wait for their decision. I am accepted and welcomed.

Were they stunned by my bold approach, so felt they had to say yes? Or were they just lovely girls? I learnt over the ensuing months and years they were indeed lovely girls. We stayed close friends throughout the rest of my time at intermediate and all through my four years of high school. I still exchange Christmas cards yearly with one of them, thirty-plus years later.

I would like to think God had all this prepared for me. Yes, I had to approach them, which wasn't easy, but it was a good confidence builder. I do believe God had these particular girls in just the right place, at the right time. I know Mum and Dad would always pray for Craig and me that we would meet and make friends easily.

I became a teenager in Palmerston North. I got glandular fever, got my ears pierced at thirteen (much drama over that decision I can tell you — so young, Sheryn). I got my driver's licence at fifteen, first real kiss ... and my heart stolen — all for the first time in Palmerston North. Many, many milestones.

One year our house was flooded because of heavy rain and a swollen river that burst its banks near our home. We, along with others in our street, had to be evacuated by the Fire Brigade. For the first night we stayed with some people at church, and then we stayed in a motel while our house was dried and cleaned.

I loved being evacuated! I loved seeing the emergency tape around our home. The drama, excitement, people helping people in need. I loved it and I loved being a part of it.

Moments like these, again, moulding my future. I see that now.

It was also in Palmerston North I made a very firm decision and decided on my future career.

So lots happened in Palmerston North. I guess from being a child and always needing to do what your parents said, to transforming and transitioning into a knowledgeable, well-lived and opinionated teenager! I was making decisions for myself.

I had to decide if I was going to smoke cannabis because my then school boyfriend did and offered it to me. I chose not to, but did buy cannabis later in life.

A biggie at the time is deciding for myself if I believe in this person called 'Jesus'. Is he the Son of God, or is this just a story my parents taught me?

Another thing I find out in Palmerston North is that life is not always fair. I had often seen this for others, but now it's starting to impact my life. And as a teenager, I don't like it — not at all.

The end of my Sixth Form year brought the life-changing phone call. Our call came early. And from my point of view it was an unwelcome one this time, that was for sure.

We were on the move to Wellington. Yes, birthplace for me, but Palmerston North was now my home. I had made a lot of very good friends. I was enjoying school and wanted to complete my Seventh Form year with my friends. I was working part time at the local supermarket. I loved The Salvation Army church I attended. I felt established. Finally, I had put my roots down — for the first time, I didn't want to move.

How can a person in Wellington just ring up and with one phone call change all that? Not fair! This was eating into the core of me that liked to be in control.

To top it all off, The Salvation Army needed Dad ASAP for a new Wellington role. He was to become the Territorial Special Efforts Secretary. A mouthful of a job that basically meant 'organise any major event that's going on for The Salvation Army'.

Why now? you ask. Well, there was a big 'congress' event coming up the following year (the General of the worldwide Salvation Army attending — like the Pope attending for Catholics. A very big deal!). And it was going to be Dad's job, along with a number of other things, to organise this. As I said, Dad is a very organised kind of guy.

Our holidays were always planned down to the last detail. Departure times, rest stops, places to visit, sights to see. Except for one time when I clearly recall Dad misjudging the distance we had to travel from point A to B. This in a time of petrol rationing. We ended up, the four of us, having to sleep the night in our car, in a playground. Suitcases made way, under the car, for sleeping bodies.

What I see now is how great my parents were at not doing drama in front of Craig and me. I don't know if they were gutted or upset by what happened, but we had the best time sleeping in a car. It became a hugely fun adventure. My kids today, when I tell them this story, want to do the same!

It was (and is!) so unlike my father to be caught out like that. He would go on to teach me that when a piece of paper comes to your desk or a letter arrives that needs a response, deal with it then and there, don't file it for later. Get it done! So, I could understand why Dad was needed to help plan this event; it's just that it was going to affect my life. I had no say in it and did not like the feeling of lack of control.

The bonus, we were told, was our family could stay in Palmerston North to see out the school year, but Dad needed to commute to Wellington every week (a two-hour drive one way), for the next twelve weeks. Again, all about me, but I liked our family being together all the time. Dad was (still is!) lots of fun. I did not at all like how this was playing out for us.

I'll talk about that difficult move to Wellington shortly, but first I want to add a side note that sets the scene for two more life stages: my Christian life and my future career.

Trust God from the bottom of your heart; don't try to figure out everything on your own. Listen for God's voice in everything you do, everywhere you go, he's the one who will keep you on track.

— Proverbs 3:5 (MSG)

Decision Time

As I've already touched on, when it came to the whole God thing, I needed to decide if I believed God was real and, if he was, what that would mean for my life. *Had I only been going to church and asked Jesus to live in my heart at the age of seven because that's how we roll in the McKenzie family?*

I invited many of my school friends to church. I think it was a novelty for some of them to experience church 'Salvation Army style'. Some would come more often than others, some not at all, but I learnt it didn't matter if they came or not, believed or not, we could still be friends.

Yes, we'd have debates about who believed in God and who didn't. Why some thought God was real, and some not. We learnt to express our thoughts and opinions while being respectful of one another.

I'm sure this small life lesson taught me about diversity and also to be confident in what I believed in. That not everyone will (or must) think the same. No matter how strong my opinion, it is but that: my opinion.

Our family didn't have a lot of money. People don't become Salvation Army officers to make money. In the world's eyes it's not the smartest career move. It's not about being rich financially; it's about being rich in seeing God bless others through you. It's a life of serving others. Anyone reading this who has served voluntarily in any capacity for any group or organisation will know that when giving to others, we feel and receive so much more in return.

Christmas Days? Yes, we would get some presents, attend church and enjoy good food together. But what was the most humbling and greatest gift? What shaped me? It was going around areas in Palmerston North to visit families who didn't have enough for extras on Christmas Day. We would deliver food parcels and presents to grateful children. Making a difference to families on what would otherwise have been just another typically, hard and stressful day of going without.

This started to teach me about justice. That life is not always fair. And that when I have the opportunity and means to make a difference to those who needed it, I should. A rewarding experience and a great lesson for this young girl: my 'normal' was only a dream for so many others.

We didn't have a lot of spare money, but that didn't matter to me and Craig. Mum and Dad, I suspect, spent many hours praying for God's help, asking him to meet our family's needs. But we didn't feel 'poor'. We were loved, happy, had a roof over our heads, food to eat, and we got one chocolate bar each as a treat if it was shopping week. Perfect. Very rich in the eyes of a child.

How God's help usually worked was that one day we would open the door and there would be a bag of groceries on our doorstep. Petrol vouchers in the letterbox. Things just 'happened' to turn up or be paid for when we needed it. Which is really how someone who calls themselves 'a follower of Jesus' operates. I would suggest we are literally Jesus's hands, heart and feet on earth — we do his bidding. This is how others helped my family. And we, in turn, helped where we could. The miraculously perfect timing and manner of the help we received, though? Just that: miraculous.

So, deep down, I knew and saw how God provided for us practically as a family. I couldn't doubt what I saw or experienced. Mum and Dad always told us how God had answered their prayers — something they had specifically asked God for, and how the answer would come.

How they felt our family had always been in the right places, right Salvation Army jobs, at the right times. With just the right friends made at each new school. *Could be coincidences, you say?* Yes, of course they could have been. But there were a lot of these coincidences, and always perfect or even better than we could have hoped for.

In Palmerston North, another significant thing happened that shaped me as a person and the beliefs I now hold so strongly. A long story, written short.

Mum and Dad became involved with a woman, through the church, who was raised by an abusive mother. The mother was heavily involved with drugs and alcohol. She also was involved in satanic occult practices and rituals.

Now, you can read what I'm going to say and think, 'Yeah right!' That's okay. I'm just telling you what we experienced and saw first-hand.

Have you seen horror films where people get 'possessed' by evil spirits? Heard those growly, scary voices? Seen people physically thrown around by evil spirits? Well, my brother and I saw that. We heard and saw it in real life, with a real person. *Scary? Of course! Weird? Yes!* But what I also saw was when Mum and Dad prayed with this woman and all that full-on stuff was happening, when the name 'Jesus' was used to tell the evil spirits to leave this woman, they did. They left and suddenly she would be calm again.

I get that this sounds strange and intense, and you don't

have to believe it, but this is my eye-witness account and would be my evidence in court. Hand on the bible.

So I could not doubt that God was real and that what Mum and Dad were doing was a helpful thing. I came to understand what the bible says, that there are good and evil spirits at work in the world. This experience shaped me and my beliefs. *How could it not?*

Therefore, I believed because I chose to believe that God sent his son Jesus for me. I believe God loves me as a good father loves a child.

One final huge, future-shaping event for me happened in Palmerston North. It decided my future career path.

One evening I'm travelling home from an event with my church youth group. We're driving along a rural road on the outskirts of town. I'm thirteen or fourteen. We turn a corner to see, on the side of the road, a house fully ablaze. We are the first people on the scene. There is no one else around. No neighbours. No fire engines.

Two thoughts immediately came to my mind. I want to be the one to ring 111 to call for the fire brigade and the police, and I also want to get inside the house to see if there were any children stuck in there.

Later that evening, we had to go to the Palmerston North Police Station to spend a few hours giving a statement to a detective. Turns out we'd witnessed a gang-related arson attack.

I loved this!

I loved the feeling of being involved in something 'exciting'. My adrenaline started pumping as I watched the fire fighters and police in action. I got a buzz out of knowing I had dialled 111 — and going to the Police Station and being interviewed by a friendly policeman topped off my night. This was the moment when I knew what my dream job was to be. (Side note: I must have had a thing for policemen and for Palmerston North. During my growing-up years I went out with two men who had been or were police officers, and finally married the third officer I dated! Something to do with a man in uniform?)

From that night on, my future career was cemented in my mind. I announced I was going to be a police officer when I turned nineteen.

I started staring at patrol cars as they drove by. I hoped and prayed Mum, Dad or I, when I got my driver's licence, would be pulled over by the Police just so I could talk to them! (A bit over the top, I know.)

I thought about my Avondale Intermediate teacher who had lost his classroom and all of his resources because of arson, wanting to make a difference to help people like him. I had (still have) a huge hatred of injustice. I can't stand it in any form. Thinking I could make a difference for people in their lives? Dream job!

My friends and family knew my dream was to become a police officer. I happily and confidently told all who would listen. To be honest, I don't think my parents took me that seriously at the start. I've never been a big person, width or height wise, so I probably didn't ooze staunch police material.

I also guess, at the time women in the police weren't in abundance. This was 1989 and women didn't make it onto the front line in the New Zealand Police until 1973, so it was still a relatively new thing.

Regardless of all this, my future path was set in my mind. But remember, we were on that unwanted move south to Wellington.

I learned that courage was not the absence of fear, but the triumph over it. The brave man is not he who does not feel afraid, but he who conquers that fear.

— Nelson Mandela

5

Living The Dream

The move to Wellington eventually happened — much to my disgust. As I've said, I do like to be in control and the decision to move to Wellington was out of my control.

I was leaving behind my good friends and a church I loved. I had also wanted to finish my Seventh Form year at Awatapu College in Palmerston North, and that option had been taken away from me. Not fair! Was I angry? Of course I was. My new, forthright decision was not to start my eighth new school just for one more year. I was done with new schools.

I was seventeen and knew I had to be nineteen before I could apply to join the police. You remember how Dad was organising that big congress event? Well, he needed a secretary. I applied and got the job — I'd like to think I got it on merit! We worked well together. Being a secretary wasn't my dream job, but I like to organise and get things done (like father, like daughter!), so it was a pretty cool project to be involved in.

A small yet important thing I remember about this time. After work some days Dad and I would drive to a lovely wee beach called Balaena Bay. On perfect Wellington summer evenings, Dad and I would have a swim in the sea together before heading home for dinner. Simple, yet I treasure that in my heart.

But despite this, I was still often being a moody, unhappy teenager!

When we first moved to Wellington, because I was angry, I moped a lot and wasn't fun to be around. I am, by nature, a happy positive, optimistic person. I'm good at hiding how I'm feeling. From the outside, I present calm and constant. But sometimes my insides tell a different story.

So I do know happy Sheryn turned into mopey, grumpy, not-fun-to-live-with Sheryn for a while. Until one day Dad said, something to the effect of, 'We know you're not happy about being in Wellington, we know you didn't want to leave your school and Palmerston North, but we are here, we are a family and your behaviour affects us all. It's not fair, but you need to change your attitude, young lady.' (No, he didn't say 'young lady', but that was the sort of talk it was.)

I didn't really appreciate hearing this at the time, but I knew it was true. I also knew I wasn't being fair on our family. It was nice to have my feelings validated, and even though it didn't change my circumstances, I started to think a very grown-up thought: that life isn't always about me.

Maybe also, when it comes to my faith, I had to consider that despite how I felt and despite what I saw, maybe — just maybe — we as a family were supposed to be in Wellington at this time.

After eight months of working with Dad and with that big event successfully over (tick), it was time for a new challenge. I applied for a job as secretary to a manager at the Bank of New Zealand. Got it. I worked there for a year. Enjoyed my time, but all the while counting down till my nineteenth birthday.

Only there was a slight spanner in the works. I discovered

the height restriction to join the police was taller than I was. Not good. But when I was eighteen, I was able to vote in my first election and the opposition party at the time, National, said if they got into government they would lower the height restriction for the police. *Great!* I don't know what other policies they had; I just selfishly decided I had to vote for them.

National became government. They made good on their promise to lower the height restriction for Police recruits. (Tick.)

Let's think about this for a moment. I want to join the New Zealand Police in just over a year's time. I've lived at home all my life. Led a pretty sheltered, blissful life. Never seen a domestic dispute, never seen violence between people other than on TV (and even that would have been pretty minor), never been into a pub, apart from in my Salvation Army uniform to sell the Army's magazine. I've never had a drink of alcohol, therefore never been drunk, never smoked, tried not to swear. I've never seen a dead body or been involved in a car accident. I still cried in most sad or romantic movies. Was I a Goodie Two-Shoes? I suppose so. But the desire to make a difference, naïvely or not, was overwhelmingly strong and had been growing for five years. It was time.

Happy birthday to me! Tuesday the 25th of September 1990. I have to say that by this stage my parents had realised I really was going to apply to be a police officer, and they were great about it. They never once told me not to, or tried to persuade me to think about other careers. They supported me wholeheartedly.

Mum did shed a few tears and sometimes couldn't hide the fact she worried about her daughter being out on the streets at all hours of the day and night, dealing with fights, drunks and domestics.

My little brother? He just thought it cool his big sister was going to be a 'cop'.

So, my nineteenth birthday. From the Bank of New Zealand in Wellington, where I worked, all I have to do is walk about one hundred metres down the road to Knigges Avenue and the Police Recruiting Office.

I arrive at my appointment feeling the most excited and the most nervous I have ever felt. This is my date with destiny. This is my moment. It is just like approaching that group of girls back in intermediate, but on a larger scale. Feeling so out of my comfort zone, but desire conquering fear.

I am so nervous. It's a heart-pounding, sweat-pooling, almost-too-much-to-bear nervousness, where I would actually feel better to turn and walk away. But no, I am determined. Face full of confidence, insides so tightly wound I can hardly breathe, I knock more confidently than I feel and march into the office of the Recruiting Sergeant.

He seems so tall — he wouldn't have needed to vote National. Solid, extremely gruff and imposing in his uniform. He also holds my future in his very large hands.

He sits down behind his desk and I stand in front of him. I am so conscious of my breathing, the loud beating of my heart and my all-important, and just passable height. *Stand tall, Sheryn, stand tall!*

He looks at me and all he says is, 'Yes?'

I clear my throat, 'Ah, hello, I'm Sheryn McKenzie and I'm here because I want to join the Police Force.'

Pause.

His eyes narrow, squint-like. He focuses as if really seeing me for the first time, looks me up and down, then laughs. Out loud. (I kid you not.) Laughs and says, 'You can't be a police officer.'

Heart sinks, blood drains from my face, despair is creeping in, my dreams are dashing out the door. But I pull them back. *Just a minute, I'm not giving up that easy!* Feel the fear, but do it anyway.

'Um, why not?' I'm gutted, devastated. *This is my moment. Was my moment. My date with destiny.*

'Well, look at you.'

I do. Quickly. What have I missed? I physically move my head to try to see what he's seeing.

Let me fill you in. I'm 165 cm, not particularly tall but not short either. I'm nineteen (and a few hours) old. I'm fit and healthy, and don't weigh much over 50 kgs, if I'm lucky. It's the early 1990s — so picture big, permed hair. I mean big! I have a lot of hair anyway, but add perming solution, teasing, mousse and hairspray. *Big!* Look, it's the '90s, okay?

I've also just come from work. Pink jacket with '90s shoulder pads, little blouse, fitted A-line skirt, stockings and a decent pair of heels. And makeup. Looking back, was I emulating a future member of the police? Given the ratio of men to women in the force then (not as it is now), he probably had a point — but the fight in me was now coming to the fore.

I may not ooze physical strength, but I know I have a strong, determined stubborn streak within. *There was going to be no injustice toward me in this room. No sir. Not today!*

'I don't see a problem, sir.'

Shaking his head, he weighs me and measures my height (my big hair did help!).

He asks, 'Are you fit?'

'Yes sir, I am.'

'Good girl. And you want to join the police?'

'Yes sir, I do.'

Head shake, again.

By the way, this is the first time I have ever been judged on how I look and how I present myself. And I really don't like it. This must have sowed another seed that reared its head later in life.

Over the next few months, I had my background checked and my parents and referees were spoken to. I sat and passed all the academic entrance tests needed for the police, and also sat and passed the required physical and medical tests.

I remember doing the required fitness level run test around the famous Basin Reserve in Wellington, where I had the pleasure of the New Zealand Black Caps cricket team, who were training at the ground that day, cheering me on. (I think it helped!)

The forms are filled in and with all my paperwork completed I have just one more thing to do. Wait for my own life-changing phone call. This one I really want. I want to be a part of the Blue Team.

About six months later, in the early months of 1991, the same gruff sergeant rings me at work and tells me I have been accepted as a New Zealand Police recruit. I just have to wait for a place to become available at the Police College. 'But inform your work you have been accepted and that sooner rather than later you will be leaving them.'

'I got the phone call! I got the phone call!' (Sing with me!)

Dancing for joy. (On the inside, of course. I'm still at work). *So excited!* What an understatement. Relief, excitement, nerves and the unknown, all competing for first place. On the outside, though, I am still employed by the Bank of New Zealand and I must remain calm.

I do phone home, bursting with pride. I think my parents are pleased. Hard to know now. It doesn't matter. My dream is about to become reality.

I was asked to choose from three places, in order of preference, of where I wanted to be posted after graduation. I was used to being told where I was going to live, so the idea of moving away from Wellington didn't faze me. And this time, at least I felt like I had some control, some say, in the matter.

My choices were: Wellington, Palmerston North, and then Christchurch. At that time no one was being posted to Christchurch, so I thought I was pretty safe putting that option down, as hopefully I would get one of my other options.

At the start of September 1991, Sir Gruff Sergeant calls again to say I am going to Police College in two weeks' time on the 16th of September. I am just about jumping out of my skin.

But there is some bad news, he says. I am going to be posted to the small town of Levin, about forty-five minutes south of Palmerston North. I don't know anyone there, so this is out of left field. He asks me to think about it, telling me he'll call back in an hour for my decision.

Very kind of him to give me all that time!

I call Mum straight away for some motherly advice. I'm so blessed to have a wise and prayerful mum. Great at listening and sharing her wisdom, but not to the point of telling me what to do. After that phone call home, ten minutes after the sergeant's first call to me, I was back on the phone.

My answer? 'Yes, I will go.'

All he said was, 'Good girl.'

I didn't particularly want to go to Levin, but this was about my dream of becoming a police officer and I had already learnt that just because you didn't end up where you thought was best, didn't mean it wasn't the right place. Plus, if I'd said no, it would have been saying no to my dream. Wasn't going to happen.

Can I encourage you? Never, ever give up on a dream! No matter what obstacles seem in your way, pursue that dream with all you have. For me, there were to be no regrets looking back.

31

I entered the Royal New Zealand Police College on Monday the 16th of September 1991, still aged nineteen. I was the youngest police recruit in our wing — wing number 127, with forty recruits split into two sections. I was given my QID — my police identification number, made up of my initials and badge number. I became Recruit SMD690.

I loved my time at Police College. I didn't know what I expected it to be like, and looking back now I take my hat off to that naïve, young girl. Brave.

I met a lot of great people from many different backgrounds and cultures. I was challenged physically, emotionally, mentally and spiritually during those five-and-a-half months. We lived onsite, in barracks, and sometimes it felt overwhelming.

But I knew God was with me. How? I felt an incredible sense of peace. *Nice, you say, but how do you know that was God? After all, you were living the dream.* True. But experiencing God's peace physically is one way I have learnt that God guides me.

While I was in training, my recruiting sergeant got back in touch to say a position had become available in Palmerston North. Would I prefer that to Levin?

'Yes please!' I said.

I could tell he was smiling on the other end of the phone. Secretly, I think he'd grown to like and respect this girl who was so determined to chase her dream.

As I said, I loved my time at Police College. The environment challenged me. The pressure was constant. The learning was new, thorough, complex and relentless. The physical challenges pushed me. Every day, something new. Every day, I would think, 'How can I possibly remember another law, another meaning, and rattle it off verbatim?'

My classmates. We bonded as a group like nothing I have ever experienced before. All there for the same reason, same goal, similar hearts. We supported one another. We were one another's cheerleaders in difficult times, helping each other whenever we struggled with certain topics or physical challenges.

Driver training, swimming challenges, being pushed physically every day, learning to use firearms, study, study and more study.

I've always felt comfortable and confident. A credit to my parents. At Police College we had to prepare and deliver a ten-minute talk on any topic. This was teaching us to be confident when speaking in front of others. I decided to talk about The Salvation Army and my faith.

You didn't? you say. Oh yes, I did! And guess what else? From week two we were decked out in police uniform. But for my talk, I decided I would wear my Salvation Army uniform! Navy black skirt and tunic, with the old-fashioned bonnet women wore back then. I stood proudly in front of my classmates and presented my speech.

I don't know what makes me feel more humble, that my fellow classmates didn't laugh, or that they accepted this young girl in her church uniform. Respectfully listening to all I had to say, not one person judging me as weird or different. I feel humbled about that even today. Despite their feelings toward someone talking about their Christian faith, which they may or may not have agreed with, they respected me. A credit to those recruits — great police officers in the making.

Yet my future almost got derailed by a male while at Police College.

Near the end of our training, the Manly Sea Eagles rugby league team from Sydney, Australia, was in New Zealand. They arranged to use the facilities at the Police College for their training.

Some of us, mainly the females, started to hang out with

them and got quite friendly. To the point where I guess I was dating one of the team. He started saying I should move to Sydney once I had graduated, since that was where he was based.

On the one hand, I had this lovely league player wanting me to shift countries to be with him. On the other, was my dream of serving as a New Zealand police officer.

Had I not been so secure in myself, flattery may have pulled me overseas. Had I not been so determined and focused on my desire to join the police, my journey would have looked quite different. We lasted a few months longer, but in the end, I was going to be a New Zealand police officer and nothing was going to deter me from that — no matter how big and lovely the deterrent!

I graduated on Valentine's Day, February 1992. It was the proudest day of my life to that point. Police College is a huge challenge, so having graduated with my colleagues, even now, causes tears of pride and relief to well up. My training was intense, journeying closely with so many good people, all with the same heart to make a difference. I will always treasure them and that time.

Heading home from college to pack my life into suitcases and move away from my family — this time, my choice. It was extremely exciting.

Two weeks later, it was time. Mum tells me she shed a few tears as she waved and watched her daughter drive off up the street and out of sight to start her new adventure by herself.

I arrived in the very familiar city of Palmerston North, driving my vehicle of choice at the time. Let's just talk about that for a moment.

I drove a jet-black VW with gold mag wheels. It sounded like the muffler was broken, but it wasn't. Picture that and let me add a few more details.

The suspension was shot, so if anyone got in the car with

me for any length of time or if I put any amount of weight in the vehicle, the back of the car – on either side — would start to rub on the top of the huge golden mag wheels. Not good.

'But the car looks amazing, Dad!' (Should have listened to Dad.)

Anyway, noisily scraping my way back into town with my VW packed to the gunnels, my life folded and tucked into suitcases, my police uniform neatly pressed in its suit cover beside me, my new adventure about to begin.

Living away from home for the first time, I was to board with a couple I'd known from my teenage years in Palmerston North. My life as I knew it, going from civilian to sworn police officer, was about to change forever and in so many unexpected ways.

Whatever you are, be a good one.

— Abraham Lincoln

Men In Uniform

The first time I lay eyes on him he swears at me. Drops the F-bomb. Harsh, loud and directed at me. Not something I was used to and not something I particularly liked. But, to be honest, I'm too busy staring into his gorgeous blue eyes to react as I should have. No smart comment. I'm left mute.

It's my first day on the job as Probationary Constable McKenzie and this handsome young policeman, QID BAD049, has just sworn at me. Something along the lines of: 'What the [expletive] do you want?'

Nice.

Little do I know that one day I'll marry this cocky young constable. *Who would have thought? I met my husband on the first day in my dream job!* (Let's just say a bit of water had to go under the bridge before a proposal was even considered. And yes, an apology for his behaviour on our first meeting was eventually offered and accepted.)

So here I am. Fresh out of college. My uniform neatly pressed and shoes spit polished. Handcuffs unused (apart from on my brother, who bore the brunt of my handcuffing practise. Yes, you do need to practise that!), and stowed in back pouch. Baton. Check. Notebook. Check. Long '90s big hair tied up and off the collar as required. Check. I am ready.

I could not have been more excited or more nervous.

Twenty-two-year-old Probationary Constable Bradley John Adamson is tasked with taking me under his wing and showing me around the Palmerston North Police Station. It's his job to teach me the ropes.

Apparently rumour has gone round the police station that a new constable has been appointed to Palmerston North from the latest recruit wing. She was the youngest in the wing, a non-drinking, Salvation Army uniform-wearing Christian who played a cornet (trumpet) in the Sally Band and a timbrel (a tambourine with ribbons). Right. Brad hasn't got the memo about me being part of The Salvation Army. He thinks I'm a 'Samaritan'. He's never even heard of The Salvation Army.

The Samaritans in New Zealand are a fantastic group of people who run helplines for people who just need someone to talk to on the end of the phone, someone who will listen and give advice. So I guess Brad was close — but not quite.

The 'Group' I've been attached to consists of one male sergeant, five other male constables ... and me. These men, of differing age, race and backgrounds could not have been more welcoming, respectful and protective.

My Sergeant, Dave Wilson (aka Sione), was about six feet tall and about the same distance wide. Yes, I've exaggerated, but you get my point. His number-one buzz hair cut was offset by a thick goatee-style black beard that came and went depending on how he shaved on the day. He called me 'Constable McKenzie' for a while, then 'Mac' for a bit, and then settled for 'Girl'. It wasn't derogatory. It was really his term of endearment for me — and I know he tried not to, but Dave probably treated me a bit like a daughter.

I was determined to prove I didn't need 'looking after' or

'protecting'. I was as capable as anyone else and was going to be an asset to the squad. I think after Dave saw me in action during a few fights he relaxed a bit. Laughed often, as he retold stories saying how I looked like a rag doll sometimes being thrown around when fighting with men twice my size, but I always hung on and got my arrests sorted. Dave rostered me to work with himself quite a bit in the beginning. *Bless him!* I think he was making sure this wee Sally girl was going to be okay and wanted me under his wing.

Colsey. Mike Coles was about sixty. No, maybe fifty. You get the point. He was the more mature guy on the squad — once we were even asked while working together if we were father and daughter. We loved that! I could not have asked for a better teacher. A lot of my policing habits and practices were formed and cemented from our time together. Mike had been a street cop his whole life. He loved it and was the consummate professional — other than the time he got bored on night shift, and as I walked out of the female bathroom in the police station he sprayed me with a fire extinguisher. Made me feel special, actually. Every newbie had to be 'inducted' and I got off pretty lightly, but it meant I was accepted.

The rest of the lads were younger, more gung-ho, and I wasn't partnered with them for some time. As I said, I think Dave was trying to protect me.

I worked in Palmerston North for about eighteen months before transferring to Wellington Central. Those eighteen months were the best training ground I could have asked for. Respected by my peers and bosses, both at work as a fellow police officer, and also as a non-drinking cop. No disrespect, but a police officer who didn't drink was a rare thing in my early days.

Sunday mornings after night shift finished, we held 'jugging sessions'. During the five-week roster, which we worked then, someone would keep a record of all the funny and dumb things everyone had managed to do. Then, at the end of the week of night shift, 0700 hours — when everyone was tired after a long night — the jugging session would begin. There would be the Jug Master and whatever he said went.

You committed a 'sin', you drank. Spoke out of turn, you drank. Held your glass in the wrong hand, you drank. (Get the picture?) It was blow-out time, wind-down time because days off were coming.

There was never any pressure on me to drink alcohol, although I did drink copious amounts of water for the sins I had committed. My skin never looked better than after those jugging sessions!

This tradition didn't only occur in Palmerston North, it continued in Wellington. But again, my fellow officers were respectful of this teetotaller. I was grateful.

Not only were my eyes opened to the behind-the-scenes of a police station, but my now twenty-year-old eyes were seeing all sorts of sights I'd never imagined. I will go on to tell you a few stories — ones that affected me deeply or shaped me in some manner. Police officers could tell stories for years. We see and deal with things 'normal' people, civilians, should not have to see or deal with.

As I've already said, we're all shaped by the experiences we have in life. Whether they're good or bad, from paths we choose or unwelcome events that simply happen to us. Every day on our journey (think about your own for a moment), the things we deal with and are involved in mould, force, push and guide us into becoming the person we are today.

Domestic arguments were a whole new world to me, making me acutely aware of the love and respect my parents share. And then there were the car chases. Some of the most legal adrenaline-filled moments of my life.

I vividly remember a car chase one evening. It starts with a domestic between husband and wife. Children in attendance as they often were, which always broke my heart. Husband and father, anger and alcohol-fuelled, grabs the family cat in a fit of rage and throws it against a lounge room wall. It doesn't survive. He then grabs his gun and takes off in the family car. Distraught mother, trying to comfort her screaming children as she calls the police.

My partner, Darren (aka Stiffy) and I are first to spot the speeding car as it disturbs the quiet night streets of our town. And so the pursuit begins. From Palmerston North, lights and sirens blazing, but there's no way this guy is going to stop. We keep our distance knowing he has a rifle on board. But we stick with him all the way to the outskirts of Feilding, about twenty minutes north of Palmerston North.

We drive all around Feilding after him, as other units try to stop him with road spikes, but to no avail.

By now we have an entourage of about five other patrol cars, plus the Feilding Police and AOS (Armed Offenders Squad). Our offender winds up on a dark, gravel back road where his car finally runs out of petrol. He and his now immobile vehicle are literally surrounded by patrol cars.

The night is suddenly deafeningly quiet as we, in our patrol cars, turn off our sirens. An eerie feeling going from full-on loud sirens, speeding cars and police-radio chatter, to nothing.

Just the quiet flicking sounds of the light bars on top of our patrol car roofs. Red and blue lights keep flashing in the otherwise pitch-black farmland and night sky.

Armed officers exit their vehicles and, protected by their cars, 'ask' the offender via a loud hailer to get out of his vehicle with his hands up. He does. Not many choices before him and for the first time that night, he chooses the correct option. Once he's lying face down on the ground surrounded by police officers with weapons directed at him, I am suddenly acutely aware of the intensity of the situation.

Aware how dangerous this job is, that I have always wanted to do. And of how desperate people can become when they can't find a way out and feel trapped in whatever life situation they find themselves in.

When hopelessness overrides reason.

Working in the police watch-house was a place to learn patience. In Palmerston North this consisted of two roles: the front desk, and the cells out back where prisoners were received and processed. More often than not, both roles done by the same one officer.

The front desk: dealing with all sorts of weird and wonderful complaints. Getting asked directions to the nearest McDonald's at 3 am by inebriated students (it was twenty metres down the road), missing person complaints, missing rat reports, lost car keys ... to the more serious reports that came in daily. Diverse is the best word I can use.

Receiving and processing prisoners in the cell block: interesting is the kindest way to describe this. Smelly, hard, sad, stressful, tiring, in your face.

Patrol units that had made arrests would drop off their prisoners, fill out the required paperwork and then head back out onto the street. Then it would be the watch-house keeper's job to fingerprint and photograph the person. Feed them if the person was staying for any length of time, especially if they were arrested over the weekend and waiting for court on Monday.

Depending on whether they were getting bailed straight away or being kept in a cell for a while would decide if they needed to be strip searched.

Strip searching someone, no matter what they had done, was an awful process. Knowing the job had to be done for the safety of all concerned didn't make it any easier. Some would yell and scream their way through the process, but still comply. Some would fight and you would need to call for backup. Such a degrading process — it was never pleasant.

The cells smelt. They were cleaned frequently, but the smell of sweat, alcohol, vomit, blood and unwashed people always remained. Wellington police cells had the same odour. The familiar smells of the cell block.

I have to say that the women, usually drunk ones, were the worst for me to deal with as a female police officer. Often spat on and sworn at, women felt they needed to put you in your place. Processing the men, you could usually get a bit of banter going and all would be done before they knew it, forms, photographs and fingerprints.

It was often the members of gangs — the younger ones, usually gang prospects — who would try to intimidate me. They were needing to prove themselves. By words, yes, but more by their actions, the way they would stand, the way they would stare at you, smirk and grin, puff themselves up. I never had anyone cross the line by physically touching me or using words that could add further charges to their list; it was all borderline stuff. As I reminisce, I know I didn't feel intimidated as a young constable. Maybe I should have. Maybe I was naïve.

I would treat each person, no matter their sex, race or the offence they were in for, with the same respect — to a point mind you. Once a line was crossed, the surprisingly forceful 'dark' side of me would appear. It's there lurking.

My kids have seen it. Not often. But it's there.

Looking at these physically big men I'd think, 'You're the one in the cell. I'm the one going home tonight. I'm in a police uniform and if you try anything towards me, a swarm of uniformed officers will be at my back within seconds. It would not be worth your while, I promise you that.' I felt safe. Rightly or wrongly, I did. I look at what police officers deal with today though and wonder if I would still feel the same. The influx of people affected by all sorts of drugs that are so readily available. Far harder to read and to deal with.

Palmerston North is full of students and soldiers, with Massey University and Linton Army Camp close by. More often than not, students and soldiers would end up in our cells because of bad, alcohol-fuelled decisions.

When an arrested person was brought into the cells, the watch-house keeper would need to deal with them. If the arrest was from a party of drunken students, friends of the arrested person would often make their way to the Police Station and stand at the watch-house front counter to buzz on its very loud buzzer. They wanted to know when their mate was being released, how long they were going to be, and could they see them. And so the alcohol-fuelled questions would continue.

On busy nights, with the cells heaving with prisoners, the watch-house buzzer under attack from impatient friends and not enough staff to deal with all the chaos, I came to understand why, on my first day, my lovely future husband felt the need to barge through the door and swear at me. He didn't find a prisoner's drunk friend that day though. He found me.

I remember near the end of my time in Palmerston North, I was asked — well, directed — to interview my first rape victim. This was usually done by a detective and none were available that evening. These interviews were also usually done by someone far more senior, but the female victim wanted to speak to a female officer. Understandable. And I was the only one available.

Three times I cried in my twelve-year police career. After interviewing this lady, I went home and cried.

The third time I cried at work was because I was handing in my resignation from the police to my boss. I didn't want to leave, but had to for health reasons. Devastated. I could not hold back the tears that day.

I'll tell you about the second time in another chapter.

Every job you attend as a police officer, no matter what it is, leaves its mark. The feelings, the emotions, the smells, what you see and how your brain processes what you are dealing with. It all starts to shape you as a person.

I never cried again when dealing with a rape victim, something I now feel sadness over. But I guess the skin started to thicken. I not only put on my police uniform as a sign of who I was, but I put on emotional armour too. I had to. A necessity, otherwise I wouldn't have survived.

This didn't mean I felt any less anger, frustration, desperation or empathy for the many victims I worked with. I just learnt to squash my normal emotions inside so I could do my job as professionally as I possibly could. Not all officers do this. For each individual it is different. But that's how I coped. (It's hard to believe now, though. As my kids would tell you, today I'll cry at anything. Movies like *Finding Nemo*, *The Notebook* — oh, so sad!)

Interviewing that woman was like interviewing my mum. A gentle, soft-featured mother, wife and grandmother who had been walking along a riverbank when she was viciously attacked. I took her statement. Listened. Asked detailed questions that I didn't want to hear the answers to. How awful and how wrong for two people, two strangers, to sit in a room and discuss the things we had to discuss.

The offender, a young man, was found guilty. This was only after the victim had to go to court and give evidence in front of him, recount what he did to her, since he had pleaded not guilty.

Do you know, after the trial, this dear lady sent me flowers? *She sent me flowers!* It was to say thank you for taking her statement and being with her on that harrowing journey. How humbling. I hated it, yet also felt (and I know this might sound weird): *this is why I joined the Police!*

I joined for times like this, when such a gentle and good human being going about her everyday life was treated so disgustingly, in a way no person should ever be treated. I joined so I could be there for people like her and try to make a difference. To journey with her and help. To try to restore a little bit of hope in humanity.

I thought I was pretty grown up in my teenage years. But this, becoming a police officer, this was on a whole different level.

These are but a few snippets of my time working in Palmerston North. In the following chapters I recount stories from other jobs I attended that shaped me or left a lasting impression. That's why I have singled each of these stories out.

But firstly, I need to get you up to date with that swearing guy, Constable Bradley John Adamson.

There are three things that are too hard for me, really four I don't understand: the way an eagle flies in the sky, the way a snake slides over a rock, the way a ship sails on the sea, and the way a man and a woman fall in love.

— Proverbs 30:18-19 (NCV)

7

Love And Marriage

I mentioned that the first day I saw Brad I truly felt something. Was it love at first sight? Probably not. Lust? Maybe. But there was something when I looked at this man. I saw past his frustrated swearing.

Cue long quiet night shifts. Good times to get to know someone. (We were very professional, just let me say that!)

I do need to clear up a couple of things — well, a couple of males — before I introduce Bradley properly, though.

Firstly, the league player I met at the end of my time at Police College. I knew deep down this wasn't going to go anywhere. As lovely as he was, I knew I needed to say goodbye.

In April 1992, I went to Auckland for a weekend to see him. I attended a Sea Eagles game at Mount Smart, now Ericsson, Stadium, and the next day we went out and I said a sad but official goodbye to my Manly friend. (Love that pun!)

As for the other guy ... (Hold on Sheryn, how many guys are there in your life at this time? *I know, just let me explain!*) ... I've already signalled that in Palmerston North as a teenager, I experienced my first real kiss. Something that actually meant something, that took a piece of my heart.

Well, that guy was about five years my senior, an ex-police officer whose parents were also Salvation Army officers.

I'm about fifteen and going to attend a twenty-first birthday party with a group of friends in Auckland. We're all from Salvation Army circles. Through camps and sporting events, I've got to know and make lots of friends from all over the country.

Saturday afternoon, we're all at a park, boys playing touch rugby, girls chatting. I spot this guy. Never met him before. A boy from Salvation Army circles going to the same party later. When I see him (say what you like, call it random, if you want to), I feel something for this stranger. He's with a girl at the time, but apparently it's a friendship in its 'final stages'. So after the party the group I'm with heads to this guy's flat. He and I talk, and talk some more. And yeah, we click.

He's twenty, I'm fifteen. He lives in Auckland and I'm about seven driving hours south in Palmerston North. He travels down to see me again a few weeks later. And a few more times after that.

I remember the night he first kissed me. Location: the front porch of our house in Palmerston North. On a Sunday: so after church, of course.

We'd gotten to know each other and I felt something for him that was different. I didn't really go out with many guys. Didn't feel the need to. I was pretty happy hanging out by myself or with friends or family. I only started a relationship if I felt there might be a point to it, not just for the sake of it. But when this guy came along, I felt there was a point. Like I said, it felt different.

Anyway, sorry for leaving you hanging on that first kiss.

Sunday evening, after church, I'm standing under the dim porch light outside the front door to my home. I'm wearing my black Salvation Army uniform, no bonnet. (*Thank goodness*, you say, *that would be weird* ... but just you wait!) I'm holding, in one hand, a handbag and timbrel case (I've already explained about the tambourine instrument Sally girls used to play), and in the other my cornet case. (Like I said, I was in the church brass band, too.) *I know! Why don't I put these things down?* But it's not like on TV when it's all perfect, slow motion and there is a director calling 'Cut!' when something is not right. This was just normal.

So I'm young, just fifteen, and maybe it's a safety factor to have things in my hands. I've really no idea. But he moves in, heart beating and ... *wow, goodbye heart!*

As he and his patient friend, who was graciously waiting in a car down the road, drive off, I heard him yell out. He sounds as happy as I feel. *Nice.*

For the next five years this guy and I dated, on and off, on and off. As much as I felt for him, and he for me, our timing never quite clicked. We were often living in different cities. Not ideal. He went overseas for some time. Again, not ideal.

I did always imagine we would sort it out and that one day it would work out for us to be together permanently. I dated a couple of other guys in the 'in-between times' during those five years, but none felt like what I had with 'Five-Year' Guy.

He knew I wanted to join the police. Didn't think this was a good idea. Fair enough. He'd been there and he knew. Protecting me, I guess.

With all this on-again, off-again stuff, the year I joined the police I made a decision in my heart and head. As hard as it was, I needed to know if we had a future. He still wasn't that happy about me joining the police. And as much as we talked, we just couldn't seem to work out a way forward together.

I ended up saying to him, 'I want you to come to my police graduation with me.' He said he couldn't. I said, 'If you don't, that will be it for me.' An ultimatum? I guess, but I needed clarity.

Like my dad, I have a bit of black and white in me, so I needed a decision. I needed direction and a plan. I didn't like this indecision anymore. Time and my life were marching on.

My police graduation? He didn't come.

I phoned a friend and she came instead. *(Thank you, Andrea!)*

There were lots of nice men at Police College. Some I clicked with more than others and, yeah, there was always opportunity to take things further. But I didn't.

Bless the boys from my wing. One evening —well, the early hours of one Saturday morning when they had been out and I hadn't — stones are thrown at my barracks window. Two in the morning, me in my PJs looking out my window and I am serenaded by about fifteen of these boys: 'You've lost that lovin' feeling / whoa, that lovin' feeling.' (Sing along, you know you want to!) It was lovely, flattering and sweet, but no, it wasn't the winning song, so I kept my heart to myself.

You get very close to your fellow recruits at college. I've mentioned it is an intense and pressure-filled environment. Like a cauldron that only you and your fellow recruits really understand. Despite all this, the only guy for me during this time was Mr Manly. He came into the picture, caught my eye, but our paths were heading in different directions.

So back to April 1992. Mr Five Years is living in Auckland again. I go to see him. We talk, easily. As we always could. I tell him about this young police constable, Brad, that I've met. I don't think he thought this really was our final goodbye. We'd had goodbyes before. But for me, this truly was the last time to say, 'We're done.' This was my head and heart moving on time.

I was sad. I had loved this man, I did love this man. And I

had thought, for a very long time, my future was going to be with him. I felt safe with him. I had never looked for anybody else. But now, despite looking at him and feeling love and loss, I sensed this was the end.

Returning from Auckland I'm ready to start dating Brad properly.

When I was thinking about writing this chapter I wondered if I should get Brad to write his side of things, or if I just say it from my point of view. 'It's your story,' he said, 'You're writing it.' So these are my thoughts ... but they have been scrutinised and cleared by Bradley. (Wink emoji.)

I had been a 'townie' all my life. This is what Brad affectionately calls me. Every place I'd lived in was large enough to have either a set of traffic lights or at least a stop sign or two.

When we'd travelled as family around New Zealand I would gaze out the window at the countryside. Seeing farm after farm, paddock after well-tended paddock, before suddenly spotting a house down a driveway — in the middle of nowhere in my books — before the farmland continued.

I would wonder, 'Who would live in an isolated place like that? What sort of people? Where would they shop? Where would the kids go to school? Who would the kids play with? What would they do?'

Well, it turns out that's the world where my future husband lived and was raised.

Brad was born in 1969 in Greymouth Hospital. A week later he was driven back to his family's home in Manakaiaua. (I'd never heard of it before I met Brad either.)

Basically, you start heading south from the stunning township of Fox Glacier. After you've been driving on State Highway 6, Haast Highway, for approximately twenty minutes you will cross the Manakaiaua River. Over a small bridge, sharp right off the highway and there is Brad's house sitting on about an acre of land. Across the road was where his grandparents lived until they died. One set of small motels two kilometres down the road, mainly for seasonal whitebaiters and tourists. And that's it.

No other people for miles. No just popping to the dairy or movie theatre. No going to visit and play with the neighbour's kids. No walking to school. Too dangerous for a half-hour walk along the State Highway to get to school. No just popping anywhere.

This is where Brad was raised — along with his two younger sisters and younger brother — by his wonderful parents, Kaye and Warner. All four Adamson children attended Jacobs River School. Its biggest attendance roll would have numbered thirty students.

Come high school, all the Adamson children went to boarding school, living at Nelson Boys and Girls Colleges respectively. Nelson, some seven hours north of Brad's family home. The children would only get to see their parents each school holidays.

Brad enjoyed boarding school. As hard as it was at thirteen to leave home, he finally had many guys his own age to hang out with. And there was rugby on offer. Brad didn't start playing rugby till boarding school, but it was clear almost from the start that he was good.

When given a job or task Brad throws himself into it utterly and completely. I gratefully see this in the way he approaches being a father and husband. And that's what Brad did with rugby and training.

After playing for the First XV at Nelson Boys, all Brad's commitment and training ultimately led him to represent New Zealand. He travelled to Australia, playing in the Under-17 New Zealand rugby union team.

Returning from this tournament, the Australian Rugby League wrote to Brad's family asking if they would consider moving Brad to Australia so they could train him in all things 'league'. They had spotted him while he was playing in Australia. Brad's mum was originally from Australia, so it wasn't such an easy decision to say no, but I'd like to think wisdom prevailed. That God had plans for Brad in New Zealand and that this is where his journey was supposed to continue. Not in Australia.

Brad played representative rugby alongside future All Blacks John Timu, Craig Innes and Walter Little. And later, while playing for Wellington, All Black Murray Pierce. He also played with All Blacks coach Steve Hanson when they both played for the New Zealand Police Rugby team. Had Brad been born some years later, when the option of making rugby a career was viable, his path may have looked very different.

But when Brad joined the Police in 1990 there was no such thing as time off night shifts or late shifts to attend the training sessions he needed to continue playing competitively. Let alone trying to work a night shift Friday and still be match-ready for senior rugby on Saturdays. It had to be one or the other. Rugby as a professional player wasn't like it is now. Brad chose his career. Lucky for me!

I should mention another development from Brad's time at Nelson Boys. At sixteen, he contracted mumps. It was more annoying than anything else, but the consequence of this virus was to play a serious part in our lives further down the track.

But back to Brad's upbringing for a moment.

Brad's mum would take her children to church once or twice a year. When a visiting Catholic priest came to their tiny yet beautiful 'local' Jacobs River Church, ten minutes down the State Highway and across the road from their school, they would attend. This was Brad's church history.

His parents have raised four amazing, well-rounded

children. I love them all dearly and thank Kaye and Warner for parenting Brad the way they have. He has had so many great opportunities because of the sacrifices they made. I love the man he is, every aspect of his personality.

For Brad, being a Christian was about going to church when Mum said, usually at Easter and Christmas. He would say he believed in God, but he would also say he believed we evolved from monkeys. Saying our ideas on a relationship with God were poles apart? Understatement.

Brad lived in Nelson after he finished high school. Worked for Westpac Bank there until he was old enough to join the New Zealand Police. (Sound familiar?) He also had a relationship with a girl for some time while in Nelson.

This continued when he moved to Wellington, but they broke up soon after he moved to Palmerston North, after about five years. Banks, five-year relationships, Palmerston North and the Police. *I know I'm stating the obvious, but interesting, aye?*

Brad moved to Wellington, still working for Westpac, but also only in preparation to get into Police College. This was while I was working for the Bank of New Zealand. We both did the mail run to the same Post Office for our respective banks, yet our paths never crossed. We both attended the same inner-city gym. Again our paths never crossing. Timing. Obviously our journeys weren't supposed to intersect. Not yet. For me, I believe this was planned. It's not some random-universe thing, but God's plan playing out for my life. And for Brad's.

So Bradley fulfilled his dream of becoming a police officer. It was either going to be that or a fighter pilot. (Let's just say he doesn't have his wings.) He graduated in 1990 and, much to his disappointment, was posted to provincial Palmerston North.

Then the buzzer went. February 1992.

It wasn't some drunken student as Brad had suspected, but 'Little Miss Samaritan'.

He didn't know it at the time, but the plan for who he was going to marry — *me!* — was already sorted. (Lucky for him, I say.) From my teenage years I had always prayed I would meet and marry just the right man for me. I know my parents prayed this for me too. For most of my teenage years, to be honest, I thought I had found that person. But no, I was yet to meet him. And in a police station.

April 1992. Brad started attending church with me. We would attend weekly bible study groups, and he started realising and understanding that I didn't just believe in God and his son Jesus, I talked to them. I had a relationship with them. I wanted to try and live by Jesus' values. I read the bible and believed it.

Brad drank alcohol and I didn't. He swore, I didn't. He was pretty blunt, forthright and confident when he spoke with people. Speaks with the head, rather than the heart. Still does. I'm more a heart person. I ask, 'How will someone feel if you say that?' Not as blunt as Brad. He wanted to sleep with me before we got married. I said no. This was hard for him to understand and difficult for me too. He'd had past relationships ... and he's a handsome man!

'This not sleeping together is not normal,' he said.

'Maybe so,' I said, 'but the only man I will sleep with will be my husband.'

Again, very secure in myself and feeling that if he really did love me, this 'gift' I had would be worth the wait and special for my future husband. Brad respected this. Didn't like it, but he respected me.

We were and still are very different, but that old saying sums us up completely: *opposites do attract.* We balance each other's strengths and weaknesses. Most of the time anyway!

A sales person will come to the door and say to Brad with a smile, 'This will only take ten minutes of your time.'

'No it won't,' Brad will reply. 'It'll take ten seconds. I don't want to buy anything, thanks. Goodbye.'

The person is often left stunned. (I cringe inside. *How must that person feel?*)

'I didn't want to buy anything, so why waste the guy's time with his spiel?'

Brad will genuinely think he's done the person a favour. Me? Couldn't do that. Not ever!

Marriage is a team game, and with lots of communication and selflessness it can be a stunning partnership. They say a champion team will always beat a team of champions. We strive to be a champion team.

I had fallen in love with Brad, but knew I could not marry someone who didn't have a relationship with Jesus as I did.

You might be asking, 'Why not? Just marry the guy if you love him. He'll do his thing on Sundays, like watching rugby on the couch, and you can go play your trumpet or whatever it is in the band and then come home, and all will be well.' Well, maybe. But not for me.

My relationship with God means I speak with God daily and trust him with my whole life. I ask God to direct my decision making. I want to do what he wants me to do.

I prayed once, 'God, if you don't want me to become a police officer, if that's not your perfect plan for me, I won't do it.' As much as I wanted to join up, if God had led me in a different direction, I would have done that. Because I trust him with my life.

And so I could not marry a man who did not live the same way. For me, I could not see our life together working with the many future decisions we would no doubt have to make. Marriage is not always easy. We aren't perfect people, and if we're not on the same page in how decisions are made? Well, disaster in my book. Look, not always, I know. I would never judge others. But for me, this was my heart's decision.

I prayed that Brad would come to understand what Jesus had done for him and how loved by God he was. My parents and brother and friends prayed too. I said to Brad he couldn't just say he was a Christian; it had to be a reality for him, otherwise it wouldn't work.

I should probably explain something. When my parents met, my mum 'attended' church, sometimes, but she didn't have a relationship with God. My father did.

Mum had a similar upbringing regarding church life as Brad. Church was a place you went on special occasions. You go, you listen, and then you go home. End of story. So Mum understood what Brad was feeling — here was this whole new thing, really not even on his radar before he met me.

One weekend, my parents drove up from Wellington to Palmerston North. Mum and Brad had dinner together and she listened and answered the forthright questions I couldn't.

Another weekend, August 1992. I was in Wellington for something. Brad phoned me late on the Sunday evening. He said he'd been to church and listened to a person tell their story about how God had changed their life. How God was real to them and guided them. Brad had physically felt an overwhelming sense of God's power, peace and his presence. He cried. (He's not a crier.) It was that evening he'd asked God to be a part of his life, however that would look.

He told me that he knew and understood how Jesus had died for him. Jesus, the holy and pure Son of God had died for Brad. He cried as he told me this. As did I and later my parents as I recounted the conversation.

And so began Brad's journey.

And having a relationship with Jesus is a journey — for me too. Becoming a Christian doesn't change you or your habits overnight. It doesn't mean you suddenly speak in 'thees' and 'thous', and never do the wrong thing. Far from it! I think people who call themselves Christians and come across high and mighty make the going pretty tough for those of us who know it's really about having a relationship with someone you want to be like, who just happens to be perfect.

Jesus is not a crutch for people who can't cope. He is literally a friend, with pretty good connections, who wants to be involved in your life. They say the people you spend the most time with are who you become like in words and actions. Well, as a Christian, spending time with Jesus is the whole point, so you become more like him.

September 1992, seven months after I first laid eyes on this young constable, we drove to Himatangi Beach just out of Palmerston North. He had prepared a picnic and afterwards, while kneeling in the sand, he proposed.

'Yes.'

We transferred to Wellington Central Police Station in 1993 and were married on Saturday the 11th of September 1993. An unforgettable day.

On marrying and changing my surname, my Police QID became SAD690. In fact, Brad and I became affectionately known as Constables SAD and BAD.

Wellington was where we wanted to be. We'd both lived there before. My parents were living there at the time. After renting and living in two different flats, we bought our first home in 1995. We've been in that house now for over twenty years. It's changed a bit since we bought it, but I'll tell you more about that in another chapter. It's significant.

So, in Palmerston North where my heart was once lost as a teenager, it had now been found and healed by another man. This time my journey back to Wellington, with Brad, was desired. It was our choice. A new life as a married couple and our career paths in the New Zealand Police beckoned. So many adventures ahead.

If you judge people, you have no time to love them.

— Mother Teresa

The School Girl

It's about 2 pm, a Friday from memory, and one of those perfect Wellington days. There is a saying, 'You can't beat Wellington on a good day.' This is one of those. There's not a breath of wind and the sun is bright and hot.

I said at the start I'd bring you back to Aro Valley some twenty years later. Well, here we are.

I'm walking up a narrow street that dissects two hills. Any breath of wind there may have been doesn't stand a chance of reaching me to give some much-needed relief from the heat. A pity. I'm so nervous I feel like I'm sitting in a sauna with a ski suit on. I can feel the sweat running down my back.

I find the house I'm looking for. Walking up the little path and just before I knock on the front door, I run my hands over my clothes, check my hair and bag. Then knock. The door is answered by a girl probably aged about fifteen. She is petite and dressed in a school uniform.

I ask, 'Is Brian home?'

'Yip,' she says and walks back into the house. She pushes the door closed behind her so I can't get a look inside. A minute later 'Brian' opens the door. He's skinny. Very skinny.

Too skinny for a man. He looks to be in his early forties and is wearing a dark top that makes him look even skinnier, with skinny jeans to match.

His gaunt, weasel-like face is moving and I realise he's asking me a question. I say to him, 'A friend told me I can score here?'

'What friend was that?'

'Just a girlfriend,' I reply.

'Well she's very naughty to say that,' says Brian the weasel.

'That's what she told me, so that's why I'm here.'

'Is she a school friend?'

'Yes.'

'Well, she's very naughty.'

'Whatever,' I say, trying to sound like a cocky, nonchalant and confident teenager, all in the one breath. 'Can I score here or not?'

'You'd better come inside,' says Weasel.

The door opens wide and he's waiting for me to step inside. This wasn't part of the plan. I don't have time to think, just react. I don't process the consequences of my actions, but my split-second decision is made. I step inside the house and hear the door shut behind me.

I'm blinking fast. The inside of this house is like walking into a cocoon. It's dark and musty; it's small and feels claustrophobic. I'm suddenly cold. I think that's the copious amounts of nervous sweat starting to dry on me. (Attractive, I know. Just saying.)

He points me in the direction of the lounge. It's dark because the curtains are pulled and the bright day outside is all but snuffed out. One tiny window, which is in the kitchen adjoining the lounge, is doing its best to let in a fraction of light. The house is right up against the side of one of the hills, so that light doesn't stand much of a chance.

As my eyes grow accustomed to the dimness of the room,

I take in my surroundings. The lounge is about four metres wide and five metres long — including the tiny kitchen. It's small, like Brian. In the lounge is an old couch and chair. On the couch are a couple of school boys and a school girl. They all look about fifteen or sixteen. The three of them are smoking and I'm finding it hard to breathe. Draped over the separate chair is the girl who answered the door.

They're all staring intently at me. I may as well be naked and standing in the middle of a busy downtown street at lunch time on any given day of the working week. I feel that vulnerable.

Brian is in the kitchen.

I reach down and adjust my bag. At the same time, I feel my ring finger on my left hand. I have remembered to take off my wedding ring. Very important in this scenario.

Let me make the situation a bit clearer. I'm twenty-two, pretending to be a teenaged schoolgirl. I'm wearing a school uniform but intensely conscious of my no-longer-a-teenager face. I'm also a police officer. I've been sent here to see if I can buy drugs off Brian, as the drug squad has received information he's dealing to school children.

Brad and I have only been in Wellington a year or so after transferring from Palmerston North, so our faces aren't yet 'known' as police officers in criminal circles.

You do get known after a while. One bonus of working in Wellington as opposed to Palmerston North is that the bigger the city, the more police officers and the more people. It takes longer to be identified and labelled. It was nice in the early days of moving to Wellington to not be 'familiar', not to be stared at by local criminals when off duty.

So my fear was very real. Hoping and praying they don't recognise me as a police officer was one thing, but pretending to be a teenaged schoolgirl put this in a whole different league! Also, I wasn't expecting that I would have to go inside the house and risk encountering people who might be more likely to sense the truth.

Brian pipes up, 'What do you want to score?'

'I just want a couple of joints.'

One of the boys says to me, 'Who's your friend that told you to come here?'

'Just a friend.' I couldn't think of anything better to say, and now I'm panicking on the inside. *What if they ask me about teachers, subjects and other school stuff I should know about?* Mistakenly, I haven't prepared for this.

Before the boy can ask any more questions, Brian calls me to the kitchen. He hands me two tinfoil joints, packed fat with cannabis.

I hand him forty dollars and give him a slight smile. 'Thanks for these.'

Brian smiles back, almost in a fatherly way.

I turn and head for the door, not even acknowledging the kids on the couch. I walk down the corridor when Brian calls out, 'Hey!'

I stop in my tracks, not wanting to turn around, 'You tell that friend of yours she's a naughty girl.' Then he laughs.

Yeah, real funny.

I shut the front door behind me and start retracing my steps back down the street. I'm blinking fast. I can hardly see, almost blinded by the beautiful warm sunlight. I love it! I suddenly remember to breathe.

I also realise I'm walking down the street with two large joints sticking out of my hand in plain view. Not a good look for a schoolgirl. I quickly put them in my 'school bag'. Just around the corner I see a car, my new target, my protection. This is the plain-clothes police car that dropped me off earlier.

I get in and say to the two waiting detectives, 'I got it. He's in the house with four kids.'

'We were getting a bit worried,' they say.

'Yeah, you and me both,' I breathe out, relieved. Pleased, job done satisfactorily. 'I'm fine,' I reassure them. 'Go and get him!'

The detectives get out of the car and head for the house. I start to relax for the first time that day. Within about fifteen minutes I see Brian walking down the street with his two new friends flanked on either side of him, his hands firmly secured behind his back in handcuffs. He doesn't look so happy now.

Once he's in the car I look at him and identify him as the man who just sold me cannabis. Brian is now doing the sweating. I smile to myself.

Things aren't always what they seem. We are so good at looking at people, making a quick judgement, putting them into some preconceived box and sticking a label on it. We then treat them and expect them to act and react in a certain way.

These four school kids and one adult looked at me, judged me to be a schoolgirl wanting to buy cannabis — yet were so far from the truth. Looking at me they couldn't really tell who I was or what my motive was. They judged me by my looks and clothes and also in relation to who they were. *She looks like us. She must be like us.*

I remember that feeling of being scrutinised by the police recruiting sergeant. *Did I 'look' like police material?* Not in his opinion.

The amount of times I attended a domestic dispute, arriving at a beautiful-looking home. From the outside, perfect. The people who lived inside must be well off and therefore happy. Once inside, a whole other story was playing out. Middle-aged professional people, yelling and screaming at each other. Husband physically abusing wife. Teenage kids hidden away in their bedrooms trying to escape what was going on between their parents.

Wife does not want to make a complaint. (*What will my friends think?*) Time after time I would see this. People living in terribly abusive circumstances, but fearing they'd be judged if people knew what was going on behind closed doors, worried that leaving might affect their work situations, worried about money, feeling it's impossible to leave.

Jesus said it rains on both rich and poor, good and bad. Domestics, pain, heartache, problems — all this comes to everyone without prejudice or discrimination. The common theme? We are all human beings.

As I've journeyed through my life, I've come to realise all of us have secrets. Things we wouldn't want others, let alone friends or family, to know about. Things that when we are alone or behind our closed doors we do, say or watch.

We get good at judging others, but only because their secrets are different from our own. Maybe you've heard of the verse in the bible that says, 'Don't worry about the speck in your neighbour's eye — check out the plank in your own first!' This is where, as a person who has a relationship with Jesus, I'm so grateful he doesn't judge me as I deserve. Because I know I'm far from perfect. I try to live and behave as I know a person labelled 'a Christian' should, but I believe it's impossible to live perfectly in the eyes of everyone. I know for myself that my ways and thoughts are far from holy at times.

The famous evangelist Billy Graham once said, 'It is the Holy Spirit's job to convict, God's job to judge and my job to love.' Often easier said than done!

I finish this chapter with one more short story on this topic of judging people, from a job I've never forgotten.

In Wellington we had until recently a very flash three-storeyed department store called Kirkcaldie and Stains.

This historic store held a prominent place in the Wellington shopping district for over one hundred years. It was not your everyday department store. You would shop here if money wasn't an issue, if you were looking for that very special gift, or if you wanted to treat yourself.

It stocked everything from cosmetics and fragrances to jewellery and suitcases. Men's and women's wear. Children's clothing and toys. Anything beautiful you could want to furnish a house, you could find it all at 'Kirks'. For a price.

On this particular day, one of our recidivist Wellington shoplifters decided he needed 'something special' for his tiny city council flat. 'Charlie', a sixty-something-year-old male, Caucasian, of small stature and build, yet strong. Dressed in a suit, shirt and tie he had 'acquired' from somewhere, Charlie looked dapper to say the least.

He made his way into Wellington City in his trusty old white van and found a car park not too far from Kirkcaldie and Stains. Charlie wasn't 'shopping' for clothes today. No, he found himself on the third floor of Kirks where all the house furnishings were. Where a huge, handcrafted, very expensive Persian rug caught his eye.

Charlie proceeded to roll up this huge rug, lugged it up onto his shoulder and then slowly and carefully made his way down the three flights of stairs to the ground floor. He made it to the store's main entry where, of course, there is a concierge stationed. (As I said, this is no ordinary department store.)

Charlie politely asks the doorman if he could please hold the door open for him. 'Of course, sir,' comes the reply.

Charlie navigates his way carefully through the ornate doors, carpet on shoulder, and heads off down the main shopping street of Wellington.

Around the corner he heads to where his beat-up old

van is parked. And then off he drives with his precious new cargo on board.

Once the theft is discovered there is much embarrassment to all parties involved. We, the police, carry out a search warrant on Charlie's home. From the descriptions given, it wasn't hard to identify this polite, elderly shoplifter. By the time we get to Charlie's flat, this beautiful rug, which took up the whole floor space of his flat, was rolled out. His furniture was all back in place on top of that rug. Charlie was loving this new addition to his home!

On interviewing him later, Charlie really wasn't that fazed. This was almost like a game to him. It's what he did. He even had the cheek to look at the boots I was wearing with my uniform and offer, 'I'll get you another pair of boots, better ones if you like, love?' *No thanks, Charlie!*

Simply because of how Charlie had presented himself, he was practically helped out of the store with his prize possession. Like Brian helping me get those drugs.

Lesson learnt. Judging people on how they look and present does not always give a true picture of who they are and the life they live. Looks can be deceiving.

We must accept finite disappointment, but never lose infinite hope.

— Martin Luther King Jr.

Not A Good Day At The Office

When I was a normal street cop we worked a five-week roster. This was made up of early shifts (0700hrs to 1500hrs), late shifts (1500hrs to 2300hrs), and night shifts (2300hrs to 0700hrs).

One week in five was called our 'swing' week. During these seven days, usually on the Monday and Tuesday, we spent time in the office catching up on our paperwork. Getting files ready for court. Ringing up victims and witnesses who probably wouldn't have appreciated a phone call during the 'office' hours we worked on night shift the previous week.

Wednesday of swing week was always a training day. This could be spent doing any number of things, from first aid refresher courses, firearms training or learning about new law changes. It was a day when we usually wore plain clothes, relaxed a little as a section, and enjoyed the day together — whatever we were doing. We had a great inspector, John Spence (aka Spency), and on this particular occasion he had planned a fun day for us.

There had been a huge spate of daytime burglaries in a well-off suburb in Wellington. So Spency had organised three plainclothes police cars for us to drive around in (petrol prices weren't like they are now!), basically to try and see if we could spring some burglars. It was a bit of fun, but we were also taking it seriously as there was nothing better than catching burglars in action.

The day was going well. We were cruising, laughing, joking and enjoying ourselves. It was good to have a breather, to let our hair down for a while.

I'm in the rear seat, passenger's side. We drive into a cul-de-sac, circle and are heading back out when our whole day and mood changed dramatically. Our driver is just cruising. We're scanning the driveways and houses when I and the front-seat passenger yell out, 'Hey, stop!'

We've both seen something that isn't right. For me, the significance of what I'm seeing doesn't compute straight away, but instinct still kicks in. I've seen something that doesn't look right and my police motto is always, 'If in doubt, check it out!'

Our driver immediately reacts. He stops the car and reverses back, questions of, 'What is it?', 'What have you seen?' flying around in the vehicle.

The person in the front passenger's seat and I jump out of the car, running down the driveway of an affluent-looking home. What had caught our attention was the garage. The roller door is down as far as it can go ... except it's come to rest on a car's rear bumper, which is sticking out of the garage.

There's a vacuum cleaner hose stuck on the back of the vehicle's exhaust pipe, leading around the car and disappearing from view. We can hear the car idling.

We quickly get our hands under the garage door and push it up. The smell hits us before anything else. Exhaust fumes have filled the garage, but more so the car. The vacuum cleaner pipe is stuck through the back window of the car and the window is shut as tightly as possible to hold the pipe in place.

Curled up in a foetal position on the back seat of the vehicle is a very small person. We can't make out whether it's a male or female, or how old they are.

By now, the rest of our carload of colleagues have joined us and everyone is playing their part, police instinct naturally kicking in.

Someone calls for an ambulance, someone calls our other two patrols to let them know what is happening, someone has called the police control room, and someone has turned off the ignition. Someone has got blankets from somewhere. No one has to say a thing. We just know what we are seeing and what has to be done.

We get the back door of the car open and carefully carry the person out.

She's a woman, aged about seventy or eighty. We can't quite believe it. She's only just breathing. We place her in the recovery position, well away from the car, keep her warm and start gently talking to her.

The adrenaline is starting to wear off a little and the realisation, disbelief and comprehension of what we are seeing starts to hit home. *How could this be? An elderly woman. A nana? A mother? Trying to commit suicide? Or is it something more sinister?*

The ambulance arrives and the section of police officers rostered to work that day also join us. We fill them in on what we've discovered, then we're 'stood down' and the on-duty staff take over. The woman is taken to a decompression chamber where people are treated for the bends, a treatment method sometimes used to treat carbon monoxide poisoning.

Our planned lunch at a café afterwards is somewhat subdued as we try to make sense of what we've faced.

The next day, when we return to work, we're filled in a little more on the tragic details. It was indeed an attempted suicide.

Though she was a reasonably sprightly elderly lady, living in her nice home, just managing to take care of herself, she had decided to take her life. Her grown-up family didn't visit much anymore. Too busy.

This woman, rightly or wrongly (we don't know what the adult children had said or done, if anything), felt she was a burden to them. She decided to take matters into her tiny, frail yet capable hands, and remove them of a 'burden' — herself.

There is much debate in New Zealand about euthanasia. *Should it be legal or not? For what sort of person: the terminally ill? the elderly? the severely disabled?* I can understand and see the different sides of the argument. This topic was raised and debated over our lunch that day.

One argument was that frail, elderly parents may feel a burden to their children, physically, emotionally and financially. Some feel if they got the home/nursing care they actually needed, it would be financially draining, which would affect their children and what they would receive inheritance-wise.

I sensed that may have been the motivation in this scenario. In itself, this was hard to think about. Feeling that this poor woman could only see one way out.

But then we were told she was disappointed that we had found her. Disappointed she hadn't been able to end her life. So now she was dealing with the guilt of being even more of a burden to her family because of what she'd attempted to do. She was living with the guilt and shame of her actions.

We went from hero to zero.

I found this hard to deal with. Not being able to comprehend how this mother, nana and sister could feel like such a burden. Again, wondering if this was perception or reality; perhaps based on things said by family members. I couldn't fathom how this lady — someone like my nana

— could reach such a desperately sad and hopeless point that this seemed to be the only option.

For so many people today, because of circumstances such as depression, overwhelming pressure, whatever it may be, suicide seems like an escape. Life on earth, for any number of reasons, can feel overwhelming for many.

This was an attempted suicide, but I've been to many when, tragically, the attempt succeeded. These jobs affected me deeply. I would wonder about the total desperation the person must have felt to get to that point. But on the other hand, I had also seen the absolute disbelief, horror, shock, grief and despair of family members left behind to cope with the tragedy.

Picking up that theme of not judging people comes into this scenario too. Until I have walked in that person's shoes, how can I say, 'They shouldn't do that', 'There is always a way out' or 'Suicide is selfish'?

Until I've walked in that person's shoes, seen life through their eyes, I can't judge. But what I know is there is practical support available.

In New Zealand, visit www.lifeline.org.nz, Lifeline Aotearoa or call 0800 543 354. If you are concerned about your immediate safety or the safety of someone else — use the emergency number and ring 111.

If life is hard for you, please reach out for help and talk about what you're feeling and what you're going through. If you think it might be hard for others, be brave and caring enough to ask how they're going. Ask if they've thought about ending their lives. Help them hang on.

My upbringing was one of experiencing unconditional love and security. And, until I joined the police force, a sheltered life.

There is a beautiful verse in the bible, Matthew 11:28–30 (NCV), where Jesus says: 'Come to me, all of you who are tired and have heavy loads, and I will give you rest. Accept my teachings and learn from me, because I am gentle and humble in spirit, and you will find rest for your lives. The burden that I ask you to accept is easy; the load I give you to carry is light.'

I think about the ways of the world and sometimes feel they are wearying. Thinking you have to try and keep up with the 'Joneses' — well, the 'Kardashians' of today! Being the taxi driver to children with day after day of after-school activities. Then the weekend is full of birthday parties and play dates and, oh ... what about homework, sport, family time ...? The list goes on.

Work is demanding. Constant financial pressures, unexpected bills. Decisions made only to realise you can't cope with the consequences. The curve balls ...

'You've been made redundant.'

'Mum,' says your teenage daughter, 'I'm pregnant.'

'I'm sorry but we've found a lump.'

... Life and the hits just keep coming.

Look, life is also a whole lot of fun and enjoyment — don't get me wrong! I love the life I have and am living and wouldn't change anything. Yes, it has had heartache and stresses. But for me, my life has a purpose. And despite my selfish ways, the mistakes I make, the bad days I have when life can look wearying, I do believe that each day I wake God has a plan for me.

Worrying about the day won't change anything (something often easier said than done). I have the choice to turn to my husband in the morning and smile or be grumpy — this will set the tone for the day. I can choose which battles to pick with my children. *Is spilling the milk by accident really something to get worked up about?*

I try to start most days spending time reading from my bible and asking God to guide me through my day. I share my worries and plans for the day. I thank God for blessings. I ask him to protect my family. I pray for friends and their needs.

Some of you will say this is just like meditating at the start of each day. Well, yes, I meditate on the words I read in the bible. I think about them and how I can apply what the bible is saying to my life. *How can these words, inspired by God, direct me today?*

For instance, Philippians 4:8 (MSG) says, 'Summing it all up friends, I'd say you'll do best by filling your minds and meditating on things true, noble, reputable, authentic, compelling, gracious — the best not the worst; the beautiful, not the ugly; things to praise, not things to curse.' *Great words, God! I need this to be my reality today. Help me with that.*

So 'praying'? Well, that for me is simply chatting with a friend. It's not about throwing my cares out there to 'the universe'; I'm sharing the start of my day with the creator of the universe. I'm talking with my friend! The one I believe set the universe, the earth and our solar system perfectly in place. It is God's Spirit who I am seeking guidance from.

Of course I get weary. I have days when I know my mothering is not at its best. I'm snappy at my husband. I eat one too many of the treats I have hidden away. I do or say things I wish I wouldn't.

But does that and should that send me down the spiral of thinking I'm a bad person, a bad wife and a bad mother? A bad person who just calls herself a 'Christian'? No! That negative little voice speaks far too loudly I think. Those negative messages: 'You're no good.' 'Well, your diet's knackered now.' 'Your kids won't forget that one.' None of this talk helps! I believe there is a plan for my life, despite how I sometimes may feel.

I wish that dear lady had felt she had a purpose. I wish that, despite the messages that may have been coming her way — both external and internal — she had felt a peace and security within her that she was living for a reason.

On that sad day, her lack of purpose taught me to love well and be grateful. To love people with compassion and respect. Give when I can, take time to listen and journey alongside others when opportunities arise. Love as I want to be loved. And be grateful. So very grateful for the life I have and those people in it who make it so blessedly full.

I'm grateful for that lesson learnt well — almost at the cost of a life.

God gave us the gift of life; it is up to us to give ourselves the gift of living well.

— Voltaire

Two Paths Colliding

Friday evening, night shift is beginning. Town, we are told, is heaving. Specifically, Courtenay Place. The strip in Wellington with all the bars, pubs and clubs. The group before us on late shift have been run off their feet. They haven't stopped attending jobs all afternoon and into the evening. Fresh incidents needing to be dealt with are backing up.

We attend 'fall in'. This is where we get briefed on the afternoon's events. What's happening in town. Which bars are busy. Where any potential party problems are brewing. Which jobs late shift hasn't been able to attend as more urgent ones have arisen.

It's going to be one of those nights, we are told. This doesn't happen every week, but sometimes a shift comes around when you go from job to job, from incident to incident all night — and before you know it, the sun is rising and it's time to go home, try and switch off and sleep.

Fall in finishes. Our Senior Sergeant says, 'Be careful out there. Be wise, make good decisions and take care of one another.'

My partner and I look at each other, smile and say, 'Let's do this.'

He. He has just finished work for the week and has headed to Courtenay Place. It's time for Friday night drinks with work mates before going home. They meet at a bar for a catch-up and wind-down time. Then he's on to the next bar to see other friends. After a while, to the next bar where word is it's two-for-one drinks.

'Sweet,' he says, 'This round's on me.'

A couple of hours later — 'Just one more bar, mate,' his friends protest. 'It's new, it has a great vibe; we have to try it.'

'Nah,' he says, 'I have to get home. The missus will be wondering where I am and I have to be up early to take my kid to their soccer game.'

'Mate! Just one more bar, a few more drinks — she'll be right, mate.'

'I shouldn't. It's really late.'

'Come on,' they encourage.

'Oh all right, just one more bar and one more round — your shout this time!'

Laughing and joking, they head for their last destination.

We. My partner and I have been attending all sorts of street disorder complaints. People fighting, a group of people rolling shopping trolleys into the lagoon, a man urinating over a shop door, egged on by his mates. A teenager stealing beer from a local liquor store. She's well gone by the time we attend. We are on the lookout during our travels for a car of yahooing kids throwing beer cans out the vehicle's windows.

Then we're dispatched to a job where people have arrived home to find their back door open and a pile of their electrical gear stacked outside the door. They are too scared to enter their home in case someone's still inside.

Off we go, along with a Police Dog Unit. If the offenders are still onsite or have only just left, a dog will be helpful.

We arrive and locate the couple. Unsurprisingly, they are shaken and nervous as they wait outside. We put them in our patrol car while we search the house. It's clear. The dog handler starts casting around outside to see if his dog can pick up anyone's scent round the property and what direction they may have headed off in.

We take the couple inside. It's disturbing and upsetting for them — as it is for anyone who has been burgled. A break-in is an unnerving thing to come home to. The kitchen cupboards are open, food is strewn all over the floor and kitchen table. Wires are pulled out where the TV and stereo system used to be. Drawers and wardrobes have been rummaged through, leaving a shambles. Tears come.

We point out spots where we will try and take fingerprints, which will hopefully lead us to an offender. 'So please don't touch those areas. But for now, let's sit down and get some details as to what has happened and what may have been taken.'

He. 'I've really gotta go now, boys. It's nearly tomorrow and the missus will be fuming when I get home!'

'Okay mate, have a good one. We'll see you Sunday arvo for that BBQ and a few more beers, aye?'

'Yeah, yeah, sounds good.'

'Hey mate, how you getting home? Not driving are you?'

'I'm not that stupid! Nah, I'm going to catch a train.'

'Good on ya! See you Sunday.'

He starts his twenty-minute slow walk to the train station.

'10/9!'

My partner and I look at each other. Standing quickly, we apologise to our burglary victims. 'We're really sorry, but that call, 10/9, you just heard shouted over the radio — that means one of our units are in real trouble and needs urgent backup.'

We don't say this, but the only code more serious than a 10/9 is 10/10. I never heard it used once in the twelve years I was in the police. I'm so grateful for that. 10/10 means the officer calling this code, if they can still use their radio, has suffered a potentially fatal injury or is in such a dire situation that without help, they probably won't survive.

10/9.

We leave our paperwork on the table, grab our keys and assure the couple we'll be back as soon as we can. But right now we have to go and help our colleagues.

Lights and siren blaring, we speed to the given location, carefully ignoring red lights on our journey. We reach a well-known Wellington pub. Outside is chaos. One of our colleagues has been bottled over the head by a drunk guy and is bleeding profusely. A sober patron is holding a towel to the officer's head and is looking after him. An ambulance is on its way.

Other patrol cars arrive from every direction. Our injured colleague's partner is wrestling with two of the offender's mates as they try to get their friend 'un-arrested' for assaulting a police officer.

A loud crowd pours out of the bar, drinks in hand, to watch the show.

Police cars and two ambulances now block the surrounding streets. Other drivers are getting angry at the road closures. They're starting to honk horns and get out of their vehicles to see what's going on. It's mayhem. You've seen it happen on the rugby field — what's been an issue between two people becomes a honey pot for bees. Suddenly everyone has an opinion and wants to 'help'.

The pulling, pushing, trying to separate parties gets more and more physical. There is the sound of bottles being smashed on the ground. The yelling and swearing volume switch has been dialled right up. Someone falls over and gets trampled. Someone else is bottled, adding to the boiling chaotic mess.

Our injured colleague is well looked after and being protected by another police officer. Closest to us is his partner, who is still dealing with the offender's mates. One of those mates is now using the officer's outstretched arm like a monkey bar, attempting to swing on it.

'That's us,' I say. Despite what some may say, this is not the time for negotiations and attempting a logical discussion about someone's unwise behaviour. No, that time is well gone. This man and the group around him are out of control.

Like hungry dogs with one bone between them, it's a frenzy of mayhem. The guy we are aiming for is trying to get the officer's radio out of its pouch for some reason. I don't think it's to call for backup.

I tackle this guy from behind, wrapping my arm around his neck to put a carotid hold on him. This means I get my arm in just the right position on his neck, elbow in line with his chin. And squeeze. That will stop the blood flow to his brain and his antics will stop. Perfect. He is grappling with me, trying to pull my arm off from around his neck. My partner grabs him too and we all tumble in a massive heap to the ground. I'm still squeezing — then peace. An effective move. We are in a crumpled pile on the ground, the three of us. Bodies, batons, beer bottles, blood, mess. I'm getting paid to do this. *What fun!*

We place the guy in a semi-recovery position, adding the security of handcuffs. We don't want him thinking he gets to go another round like Mike Tyson when he wakes.

After about ten minutes of adrenaline-filled chaos, order is restored. The goodies have won (that's the police!), the injured have been bundled into ambulances — our colleague included. Those who have well overstepped the law are helped into patrol cars and returned to the Wellington Central Police Station.

The bar manager is being spoken to: 'Your patrons are too drunk!' There will be a follow-up on this matter.

He. On his laborious walk to the train station he passes the Wellington Central Police Station, walks into the watch-house and starts pressing the counter buzzer to get some attention. One of our watch-house keepers comes out to speak with him.

'I'd like a ride home.'

'Where do you live?' North of the city centre.

'You know this is a police station, not a taxi rank?'

'Yeah, I know, but I need to get home.'

'And how did you originally plan on getting home tonight?'

'I was going to catch a train, but I've spent all my money on booze, I can't find my credit card and I'm too tired to walk. I really need to get home — the missus is going to be so upset with me.'

'Well, we can't give you a ride home. It's Friday night, we're short staffed anyway and busy.'

So how can I get home?'

'Call your wife?'

'I've got kids, mate. She'd have to get them out of bed and bring them into town. It's not worth my life.'

'You should have thought about this a bit earlier. You're a grown man, a father!'

'Yeah, I know,' hanging his head and rubbing his hands through his hair.

'Look, we won't be able to take you home, but I'll see if one of our units can take you to the station and I'll give you some money so you can get home.'

'Oh, cheers, thanks mate!'

The watch-house keeper puts a call through to our

communications section to see if there's a unit nearby to take the guy to the train station.

We. Two units are leaving the police station. We need to head straight back to our burglary couple who we left hanging an hour or so ago, so the other unit responds, 'We can take the guy. We're heading north towards the train station. Send him out the front and we'll be there in one minute.'

The watch-house keeper passes on the good news. 'Okay mate, you head out the front and one of our cars can drop you at the station.'

'Thanks so much mate. I'm so grateful! The missus, see, she's going to be so angry — I'm taking our kid to soccer in the morning. My head's going to be a bit sore.'

'Yeah, well, you've made some poor choices tonight and got yourself in a bit of a state, so get home and sleep it off.'

He. He had his last pint tonight. Ever. He won't make it home, despite having the money and the means. He won't ever see his angry missus, nor will he be taking his child to soccer. Not ever. That Sunday BBQ with his mates? Cancelled. He will make one more bad decision tonight.

We. We finish with our burglary victims. They've calmed down and realise they have been very lucky. No one has been hurt. They still have their property and can clean up the mess the burglars left. They understand why we had to rudely race off mid-discussion. We reassure them it's unlikely the offenders will be back. We discuss getting better locks on the back door and say our farewells. They start the job of cleaning up their home, while we head back out to keep cleaning up the streets.

It's now the early hours of Saturday morning. We have been working solidly since we left the station at just after 2300 hours.

We say over the radio that we are K-6 10/3, which means

we have finished our last job and are free and ready for another one. Our sergeant comes on the radio and calls us to meet her.

'I'll see you at the train station,' she says.

He. He had been dropped off at the train station. Personally given enough money by our watch-house keeper to get the train home.

'Your train will be here in twenty minutes.'

'Thanks again, mate!'

After waiting about fifteen minutes, CCTV footage shows he got tired of waiting and decided to walk home after all. Bad decision.

He steps down off the train station platform onto the railway lines and starts heading north on the train tracks towards home. About thirty to forty metres down the track, we watch the footage as he stumbles, corrects himself, then stops again. Lies down between the tracks and, using the steel train track for a pillow, goes to sleep.

Just minutes later the train that would have taken him safely home arrives on schedule.

He is asleep on the line. Dressed in his dark work suit there is no lighting down where he is sleeping. Impossible for the train driver to see him. To avoid him.

He and we meet. Along with our sergeant, the train inspector and an ambulance crew.

Railway staff use a machine to jack the train off one of the lines. It's balanced on its side so my partner and I can climb under the train, over one side of the track to the other. Some of him is still here, but not all.

We have our torches in one hand and a large plastic bag in the other.

Amongst other trauma, he has been decapitated by the wheels of the train.

The first thing I come across is some of his head and hair.

I put this in the large bag I'm holding. For the next fifteen minutes, by torchlight, my partner and I — along with our sergeant who has joined us in this gruesome task — search under the train along the tracks for every part of him we can find. It is surreal. I cannot and do not allow myself to think logically about what I'm doing. I don't know if I would cope.

No human should have to pick up pieces of another human while wedged uncomfortably under a train in the middle of the night. It's not normal.

After fifteen minutes my partner and I are replaced by colleagues from another unit. They crawl under the train and say, 'Have a break, we'll take over.'

'No, it's all right, we'll keep going.'

'No,' says our sergeant, 'we are having a break.' When I start crawling out, relief sweeps over me and I realise I'm grateful for this break after all.

I'm sweating even though it's not hot. I feel cold. I see blood all over my uniform, and not from the fight earlier in the night. I can feel my knees are bruised and raw from crawling over rough tracks and stones. My back aches from being hunched over in such a tight space and I notice I'm smelling what I recognise as smells humans make when they have died.

We hear sobbing in the distance and see the train driver being comforted.

We also hear, over the police radio, that a unit has been dispatched to speak to the man's family, carrying the devastating news that he will never come home. Someone else will have to take his child to soccer games. But not this weekend.

After we have done all we can at the scene, we drive back to the station. It sounds terrible, but my partner makes the joke, 'Well, he won't do that again', and I laugh. It's terrible because this is tragic, not funny at all. We both know that, but we are laughing anyway.

I'm just saying how it is —please don't judge me until you've walked in my shoes. If my partner didn't make that joke, I probably would have started to cry. Maybe he sensed that. We still had the rest of our shift to get through.

My partner is a father who is also planning on taking his boy to soccer later that day, after a few hours of sleep. He was complaining at the start of the shift that he would be tired at his son's Saturday game. I know now he's just grateful he will be there.

We laugh.

It's how we cope. It's not normal, what we've just done. Our minds are battling between being a police officer with our game-face on, and being a normal human being who has just picked up pieces of a father's body from underneath a train.

We are keenly aware of the devastation now unfolding in a quiet suburban home.

Cleaning out a cupboard recently, I found a folder of all my old police appraisals. Flicking through, I found one dated 03/12/19--. My senior sergeant had written, 'Sheryn attended messy 1S (the code for a death) at the Railway Station.'

Yes, it was physically messy, but now I remember that this husband, father, friend and son had died just before Christmas. Messy indeed.

After this event, those of us who attended were required to go to a psychological counselling session, all together, because of what we had seen and dealt with. Beforehand, the guys didn't want to go and laughed they didn't need to see a shrink. But there wasn't any laughter during that session. Quite the opposite.

Life is all about choices and decisions, and these days I'm learning to stop the 'what ifs' in their tracks and just make the best decisions I can in the moment. I'm about living and enjoying each day. Living in the moment with the people I love and care for. Being grateful for even the smallest things. Remembering the 'be grateful lesson'. Enjoying the day, whatever it brings.

King Solomon, son of King David, who hung out with the Queen of Sheba and was reputed to be one of the wisest men who ever lived, made some wise and pretty down-to-earth statements about life and the futility of it. 'Young man (young person), it's wonderful to be young! Enjoy every minute of it! Do all you want to: take in everything, but realise that you must account to God for everything you do. So banish grief and pain, but remember that youth, with a whole life before it, can make serious mistakes' (Ecclesiastes 11:7–10, TLB).

Wise words.

We make decisions every moment of every day. Sometimes thinking about the 'what ifs', sometimes not. Lots of small choices happen almost without thinking. Some we spend more time over. Sometimes the decisions we make without thinking have us looking back in hindsight shaking our heads. *If only.*

When two paths collided that night, I was reminded of the drastic consequences some of our choices and decisions can lead to. This lesson has stuck with me because it played out so tragically and vividly, right in front of my eyes.

Death leaves a heartache no one can heal, love leaves a memory no one can steal.

— From an Irish headstone

First Impressions

The start of late shift. The first job is being dispatched.

'CTI from coms.'

'10/3 central city.'

That's our communications centre calling us. We, in return, give our status and location so the dispatcher knows we are free for a job and are in the central city.

'Copy. Stand by for job details.'

'Go ahead.'

'Proceed to ---- flats where you will meet with the property manager. He reports a bad smell coming from a certain flat and the occupant hasn't been seen for a couple of weeks.'

'Great,' we think, knowing other patrols are thanking their lucky stars they didn't get the job. The usual and probable outcome of a job like this is locating a body that has been there for some time and decomposition has started. A sad eventuality that happens all too often.

My partner and I look at each other. Because it's the start of the shift we haven't decided who will take the first job. Yes, we'll work it together, but one person will have to be O/C (officer in charge). We chop for it.

Paper, scissors, rock. Draw.

Round two: *Paper, scissors, rock.*

I smile, 'Sorry.'

We arrive at the address and along with the embarrassed property manager —he can't find the flat's spare key —head up to the third floor. Pretty soon our noses are working overtime. The smell even from twenty-five metres away is putrid, like putting your head in a rubbish bin without being allowed to breathe through your mouth.

The stench when standing outside the door ... well, we are gagging already and we aren't even inside yet. I pull out some trusty peppermints and we pop one each in our mouths — it helps with the smell. Because our apologetic property manager hasn't got a key, my partner has to smash a small glass panel just to the right of the door handle and lock.

It almost looks like it has been made with this situation in mind: 'In case of lost key, smash glass panel to the right, reach hand inside and turn lock.'

We knock on the door, 'Mr ----, are you home? Hello, it's the police, open up please.' We wait for some time, knocking, waiting, breathing through our mouths.

Nothing.

My partner uses his wooden baton to smash the window.

Once the glass is broken, the smell has an escape route. It rushes out with all the force it can muster after being trapped inside for so long. So strong it literally makes us take a step back. But we've done this before, we know what to expect, and so with gloves on we ready ourselves for what lies beyond the door.

My partner — he's been around a while like me now — puts his hand through the newly made entrance porthole and reaches his hand in, carefully, as far as it can go, to unlock the door. As I said, he's been around a while. He's not some flighty scared guy. But what happens next makes me start laughing.

My partner suddenly lets out a half yell, half scream and retracts his arm quickly from the hole. 'Someone's just grabbed my arm!'

He looks at me a little horrified, then a little embarrassed as I'm still laughing at his reaction. I know I would have done exactly the same, but he was the lucky guy to lose the 'chop' so this was his job.

We'd forgotten about the smell, just for a moment, until the door is opened very slowly, very timidly. The hot, foul, putrid smell continues to ooze out to fill every pore of our beings and the fabric of our clothes. The property manager has positioned himself behind and well away from us. I don't blame him. A wee frail man stands before us. He is filthy. His clothing is filthy. His flat is filthy. But he is alive.

The heat is almost as unbearable as the smell. Curtains are closed, a swarm of dirty-big blowflies are having a party in the kitchen area and another group has started their own party in the lounge area of the tiny flat. So now we have hot thick air, combined with the foulest of smells and loud buzzing for sound effects. Not fun or funny anymore.

We discover that our frail gentleman, with no family to check on him, hasn't left his flat for two weeks. His cat died. We see that now. What looks like it was once a cat is on the lounge floor lying on a blanket. It's dead, but it's moving. An interesting but horrific phenomenon. (It's the maggots, you see. And that's all I'm going to say about that!)

'My cat, he was my best friend. I think he might be dead.'
'Yes.'

Inside you want to say 'no kidding!', but of course we don't — this is our profession. But that's how we debrief later. It's how we cope with what we work with. It's not funny; it's tragically sad that a person just like my dad, your dad or granddad, can find himself in this dreadful situation. If you don't laugh, you would cry — and cry a lot. So, we laugh, but later. And not because it's funny. But right now, my partner has a deceased yet still moving cat to deal with.

The kitchen is rancid, with mouldy food on the bench and dishes in the sink. The rubbish bin is overflowing and a brief glance in the fridge confirms it's not in pristine condition either. We check the rest of the flat to make sure there's nothing else to be discovered.

The dear man offers us a seat and a cup of tea. We politely refuse both. We enquire about his heater, which we have managed to locate and turn off. 'Oh, I was hoping the warmth would help my cat, I thought he might just be cold. He wasn't moving and I thought it might help him wake up.' Nope, didn't work.

This story ends well, apart from the cat's demise, of course! The man is taken into care, his flat fumigated, the glass repaired, manager grateful, and another tenant moves in.

This time we were welcome faces. When that man saw our uniform he was happy and knew we were there to help. A good first impression, despite us having already made a judgment call on what we thought we were going to be facing!

Later in the same week, same partner, different job. Job details for an advising job. It was our turn to deliver some terrible news.

Advising jobs are more often than not the hardest and saddest jobs in the police. It's when you need to advise family members that someone close to them has died, usually from some form of accident.

The call came at the start of our shift. *Paper, scissors, rock.* All I'll say is I'm good at this game. My partner sighs.

He phones the communications person and they give

him the details. It's not broadcast over the police radio — far too many people can listen in. He looks at me: 'Car accident, sixteen-year-old boy, passenger — and it looks like his mate was drunk driving.'

I shake my head. The terrible news we have to deliver is going to change a family's life forever.

We drive to the address in silence. It's times like this in the police you don't enjoy, at all, what you do. The sobering side.

The side, when you pull over a drunk or dangerous driver, that makes you feel anger. Anger because you've seen the results too often. Not just the results of the physical crash. Shock, chaos, then drugs from ambulance officers often means the injured don't have to deal with the carnage around them. But the horrific and real results for the families away from the scene who need to be told — for those who will have to continue living with the grief.

People often talk about 'just knowing' when they open their door to find a uniformed police officer standing there.

Sitting in our patrol car outside the address we check ourselves in the car mirrors to make sure we look professional. Hats on. I look at my partner, 'You okay?' I've done this before and I know he's feeling nervous, a bit anxious. Not wanting to get out of the car because he is going to ruin a family's life. Once the door of that home is open and the conversation begins, there is no going back. Life for that family, from that moment forward, will be and look different, in a bad way, forever.

He's also feeling grateful. Grateful it's not his family. Grateful we don't know the victim, although this only helps a little bit. He's rehearsing in his mind what he's going to ask and say.

Every person reacts differently. Once you have delivered the news ... well, sometimes you don't even have to deliver the words. The sight of two police officers standing solemnly at your door late in the evening is usually enough, as I've said. But once the devastating words are out you pretty much follow the lead of how the family reacts. What questions they ask and what they need.

We are standing at the front door and my partner sighs, looks at me with a sad smile and knocks. 'Here we go.'

A man, the father, comes to the door. Looks at us as my partner makes the introductions. Immediately, a woman, the mother, comes to the door. As she sees us, she pushes her husband to the side, looking frantically between our faces.

There are no words, our faces tell the story. My partner asks to come inside, but the mother yells, almost crazily, 'Show me your ID cards!' We are standing there in full police uniform with a patrol car parked directly behind us, just a few metres away on the street. But she is already going into shock and doesn't want this to be real. She is not wanting to hear what she thinks ... *knows* ... is coming.

The father says, 'Don't be stupid. Let them in, it's the police.'

My partner repeats, 'We need to come in and speak to you please.'

In a fraction of a second we see shock, horror, understanding, grief and anger cross the mother's face. Her response? She punches my partner in the face. No word of a lie. Right fist in my partner's face!

This well-to-do, fifty-something-year-old woman punches my partner. She's probably never punched anything in her life, let alone a person, but now she's dealt to a police officer. *Shock.* The husband grabs her as she starts crying and gently pulls her inside. We follow — after I check my partner's face for blood. He didn't see that coming! I've never seen a reaction like that before. Like I said, everyone is very different.

My partner's not angry. Stunned, surprised and still gutted he lost the chop, that it's him delivering this news, not me. But he's not angry. The minor damage done to him will heal. There won't be healing for this couple. These parents have just lost their sixteen-year-old boy. Their lives are changed forever because of someone else's bad choices.

My partner didn't even need to say anything. The sight of our uniforms and faces told this woman the story. Judgment calls made within three to five seconds.

I remember finishing up one afternoon at someone's home after taking a burglary complaint. My partner and I are walking down the path to where our patrol car is parked on the street. There we see our sergeant. Parked next to our vehicle, waiting. She gets out of the vehicle and has 'the look' on her face. I have worn 'the look' before. A few paragraphs ago I described my partner wearing 'the look' — and he got a punch in the face for it.

I'm hoping the look isn't for me. Sadly it is.

My sergeant delivers the news that my grandfather has died. I flash through the stages I have seen others work through before. A moment to comprehend what is said ... disbelief, shock, sadness ... then tears. I hold my tears back. I am still on duty. I am standing there in my police uniform, so this is not a time for tears.

'Are you okay?' asks my sergeant as my partner puts her hand on my shoulder.

'Yeah, I'm fine. I might just head back to the station, finish my paperwork and then go home, if that's alright?'

'No Sheryn, that's not okay, I'm taking you home to your family. You're finished for today.'

The tears well again. The compassion of my sergeant and partner overwhelm me. She is taking control of a situation when this is usually my job with others. This time it is my turn. Despite what I am wearing, the reality of being a loved granddaughter overwhelms me and my blue uniform is forgotten. My outside picture of strength doesn't represent my growing grief and loss inside.

Sometimes pain in this life comes through our own poor decision-making. I talked about that in the last chapter. Sometimes, as it did for those grief-stricken parents, pain comes through another's bad choices. But sometimes there is pain because we have loved.

I thank God for the relationships I have formed here on earth. Relationships are for a reason. And despite some of them being disrupted by death in this 'chapter' called 'life', there is another chapter yet to come, where those bonds will be restored — completely, wholly and forever.

Do not judge. You don't know what storm I've asked her to walk through.

— God

Come On Light My Fire

For the first six years of my policing career I was a normal 'street cop'. For the second six years I worked with a small specialised group that conducted covert work.

We were attached to the Organised Crime Squad. So, without going into too much detail, it meant we would watch criminals. We would gather information on what they were up to, who they were meeting, what houses and places they would visit. And often we'd watch them while they were committing crimes — obviously not ones where people were getting hurt! All the while, they wouldn't know they were being watched. That's all I can say and am going to say about how we operated.

This was one of those jobs. We had received information that a young teenage female was leaving her home at night, wandering around business premises and randomly choosing buildings in which she'd light fires, thereby committing arson. There wasn't enough evidence to progress any further, so our team was called in.

We were given the address of the suspect and details of the approximate times fires were being lit.

One evening our team started watching the girl's home.

Sure enough, about 12:30 am, we see her walking out of her driveway. She is wearing dark clothing and a small pack on her back.

I take off my police hat for a moment to put on my concerned citizen hat, and wonder: *Why does a teenage girl feel the need to leave home in the middle of the night to light fires? What is happening, or not happening in that home that causes her to do this?* I get frustrated thinking about this, wondering: *What is the answer? It's certainly not putting her up before the courts to deal with, but that's what will happen.*

I put my police hat back on.

She wanders into an area with a number of shops. It's well lit and we can easily watch her just looking in windows and strolling around. After an hour we begin to wonder if she really is the arsonist or if she's just a bored young girl who likes to wander the streets.

However, about 1:30 am she heads out of the main shopping area and walks down a number of streets, arriving in a part of town with lots of industrial buildings and not a lot of street lighting. Cars are few and far between and there are no other people around. It's very deserted and dark.

I am starting to get a little excited ... or is that the wrong word? I choose it carefully because I mean it — *I want her to light a fire! How terrible is that?*

I'm only speaking for myself here, not those others I was working with, but it's 1:30 in the morning, it's cold, I'm tired, and seeing this girl starting to show signs she might be the one we are after ... well, I really want her to do it!

I'll talk about those feelings again. Back to the chase ...

It seems she has chosen a street that appeals to her. Again, it's dark, deserted, lots of those industrial buildings, plenty of them wooden. She has spent about fifteen minutes wandering this street, starting to smoke a cigarette as she walks.

Now, because it's the early hours of the morning and we're in an isolated spot, you can imagine there aren't many cars around. The group I'm working with, we are all in separate cars. We cannot keep driving around to watch what she's up to as we'll probably scare her off.

So our next challenge is to find somewhere where we can watch what is going on without her being able to see us.

I see a spot that might work. Parking my car quite some distance away, I get out, quietly close the door and start walking. It's dark and cold. Dew is setting in so the ground is damp. *Good thing:* I've found a perfect place to watch her from. *Bad thing:* it's under a big hedge, lying on the ground in some random person's front yard.

I'm wearing warm clothes, I've got a radio/walkie talkie in a backpack and an ear-piece in my ear so I can communicate with the rest of my team. I creep across the unsuspecting person's property. Kneeling down and then crawling on hands, elbows and stomach, I bury myself under the hedge. It gets thicker and denser the more I squeeze under it, but finally I'm in place. My head is just back from where the hedge finishes and where the footpath starts. Straining to look back, I can see that my feet are just poking out of the thick hedge, so if the owners do happen to look out their window at 1:45 am, they may see a pair of shoes sticking out of their nicely-trimmed hedge! I silently pray they don't wake.

Anyway, I'm stuck under the hedge, it's dead quiet and I whisper into my radio that I'm in position and can see our 'target'. I'm not comfortable, but my adrenaline is pumping, so I don't feel too bad.

Half an hour later, I'm still lying under my hedge and, yes, now I'm feeling bad.

I have been watching the target continually wandering up and down the street. She sometimes walks towards a building, has a look around, but then walks back out to the footpath, scanning up and down the deserted road.

I'm lying as still as I can. Waiting, watching, hoping. I'm very cold, uncomfortable and now wet too. It feels like the damp earth is trying to leech its way through my layers of clothing and play havoc on my skin.

Suddenly I stifle a scream. My heart leaps into my mouth as something brushes over my feet. An inquisitive cat has come to inspect this new thing squeezed under the hedge in its garden. I didn't notice or hear it until it tapped its paw on my leg and stepped over my shoes! I truly just about have a heart attack. I manage to get my breathing under control and concentrate on the matter at hand while politely telling the cat to shoo!

The girl heads back to the building she has spent the most time hanging around. It's a wooden one. Another cigarette is lit. I watch her walk to a corner of the building. I can see her flicking the lighter she is carrying. All the while she is doing this, I'm relaying via my radio, very quietly, what I'm seeing to the rest of the team. I am their eyes. I know everyone is hanging on my every word — we're all waiting.

I watch her walk up to the footpath for one more look up and down the deserted street before returning to the same spot. She's flicking her lighter, again and again. Bending down to a corner of the building, I see her flick her lighter, before she quickly stands up. She looks out at the street one more time, then turns and crouches down again ...

My heart is pounding. *This is it! She's going to do it. All our waiting has paid off.*

Lights, headlights. A car has turned into the street. It destroys the quiet, deserted nature of our surroundings and I see our girl duck out of sight, her lighter well and truly extinguished.

The car, a taxi, drives past the building she is hiding

behind and disappears from the street. After a few moments I see the girl get up from her hiding place, walk back up to the footpath and then, walking at the quickest pace and taking the most direct route we've seen her take all night, she heads back home.

To say I am gutted is an understatement! I am disappointed she didn't light a fire.

Thinking about this later, I realise I hadn't really wanted this particular young girl to light a fire and have to deal with the consequences of her arson. (I'm not that terrible a person!) I was cold, wet and tired and simply wanted a result for our night's work! I selfishly wanted that result no matter how it was going to come about. I wasn't thinking about the consequences for the girl.

By the way, that girl did light a fire some weeks later. She was caught, dealt with by the police and got help.

I tell you this story because it shaped me, causing me to think about myself and my motives.

I felt (and still feel) ashamed when I think about the disappointment I experienced when that night didn't go as I wanted. Some police jobs stick in my mind for different reasons. This one, yes, partly because of the hedge and the cat moment, but more so because of my selfish thoughts. *It's all about me!* I wanted that girl to light a fire so *I* could get a result.

I like justice. I felt I'd played my part, but she hadn't played hers. (Warped, I know, but I hope that on some level you understand!)

This leads me on to a story in the bible, from John chapter eight. It's a story I love, but that always makes me angry when I read it.

During the time Jesus was hanging out on earth, he was in Jerusalem one day. Some religious people brought a woman to him who had been caught in the act of adultery.

These religious people had exposed her and demanded justice. Because in their minds she deserved to be punished.

No real thought about the woman. Certainly no compassion. I bet when she was 'caught in the act' she was dragged out of the house, probably not even dressed, but no thought would have been given to the shame or embarrassment this would have caused her.

For me, the obvious question, the elephant in the room, is: *Where was the guy?* He's not even mentioned. Why wasn't he dragged out, since he was also 'caught in the act'? We all know the saying it takes two to tango, right? In fact, I'm getting my back up now just writing about it. *Such injustice!*

So these 'religious' leaders bring this woman to Jesus and tell him she's been caught committing adultery. They remind him that the religious law of the day says she must be stoned to death. *Now, what are you going to do about it, Jesus?*

So ... Jesus ... to some of you, a good guy with good morals. (Fair comment.) A prophet, a hippy who had long hair, wore sandals and robes, and had some good one-liners and ideas to live by? Maybe a crazy guy who claimed to be the Son of God and whose life is written about in a book called the bible that may or may not be true. I know some of you will think that. Others are thinking: holy, perfect, son of God. (Another fair comment, one I agree with.)

But Jesus, no matter what we think of him, stands up for this woman. Does he throw a stone? No. Instead he has a brilliant one-liner for those religious guys: 'Let any one of you who has never sinned be the first to throw a stone at her.'

Outstanding comeback!

What Jesus dealt with still happens today. What did Jesus do? This good man, this prophet, this hippy, crazy guy, this son of God? Jesus had enough courage to stand up to the crowd. He didn't back down and support what was going to happen. He, a man, stood up for a woman. Especially stunning in those times.

Pretty great friend to have — so pleased to say he's mine!

Yes, this woman had done something wrong. Committing adultery is wrong. It hurts people. Adults and children alike. But wow, who doesn't do things that hurt people sometimes? I know I do, but I also know I'm pretty good at justifying all sorts of behaviour in my mind when I want to.

Does Jesus condone what she'd done? No. After his great one-liner the stones are dropped, one by one, and all the men walk away. So now it's just Jesus and the woman. And he says, 'If no one condemns you then neither do I.' But — and there is a but — 'leave your life of sin, stop what you're doing, it's wrong. But I'm not here to judge, and my message to you is: *I love you more than I hate what you are doing. I'm here to give you a way out.*' (I've used some of my own words here, but it's the gist of what Jesus was saying.)

Jesus knew what she'd done in 'secret' (as well as what the unknown man she'd been with had done). God sees what we all do in secret. Yet loves us still.

Miss Arsonist had a secret. She thought no one was watching. Did she know her actions were wrong? Her behaviour when the taxi drove past proved she did. Her motive? I don't know. As I alluded to at the start of this chapter, was it attention seeking, boredom, a cry for help? I don't know her 'backstory'.

And this is where the difference lies.

God knows everyone's backstories. Why we think, feel, act, react, speak, laugh, cry, and behave the way we do. God saw how disappointed I was when Miss Arsonist didn't light that fire. He sees where that sense of perceived injustice came from within me. And God knew why this young girl left her home, on a cold, dark night, by herself, to light a fire.

God saw where the desperate need for the woman caught in adultery came from.

We all have backstories. Some we are happy to tell, some stories are only told to those people we trust, and some of what we've done or thought we hope will never be discovered by anyone. Because Jesus knows all and sees all about us — about me, about you — he doesn't throw stones. He reassures us that he gets it and looks at us with compassionate eyes.

I needed to learn a valuable lesson that night. Sometimes I just need to drop my stone and walk away. And I need to be okay with that.

Above all shadows rides the Sun.

— J. R. R. Tolkien

Heartbroken Child, Heartbroken Cop

This chapter will be a hard read. It was hard for me to write, to read and to re-read. But what I'm about to recount affected me deeply, scarred me and shaped me hugely. You might even need a cuppa for comfort.

Let me introduce you to a four, maybe five-year-old girl. I can't remember her name, and even if I did, I wouldn't use it. So I'll call her 'Mary'. Some details are sketchy; some are as vivid as if this happened just yesterday.

Our section was working the early shift, starting with 'fall in' at 0645 hours. We were briefed on what happened overnight, what jobs are outstanding and other matters to be aware of. We were then assigned our patrol units. I was to work on my own, so was mainly expecting 'reporting jobs'. For example, taking burglary complaints, attending minor car accidents, or other general enquiry jobs that will come in during the day.

Little did I know that this particular day would turn out to be one of only three times I cry during my twelve-year police career.

I've talked already about going home after interviewing my first rape victim. I've briefly mentioned crying the day

115

I handed in my resignation from the police. But crying on the job, not later in the privacy of my own home when my uniform was off, but actually at a job — this was today.

Early afternoon I get a call to return to the station to see my sergeant, Andrea Jopling. She was one of the best sergeants I would work for and I had (and still have) the utmost respect for Andrea. Great police officer, great lady.

The details of the situation are now sketchy to me, but basically a custody dispute has been under way for some time and, with a court order signed, the moment has finally come for four-year-old Mary to be taken away from a loving grandmother and put into the care of her birth mother.

The grandmother has raised Mary for most of her short life. In Fiji. Mary's grandparents are well off and respected Christian people in their community. Mary's mother — who very early on gave her daughter to be raised by the Grandma — now wants Mary back. Mary's mother has not seen her child since she was placed in her own mother's care.

This is where I can't remember the details of how or why it had come to this. But legally, the courts have ruled that Mary must return from Fiji to live in New Zealand with her mother, who has been granted custody.

My sergeant informs me that she and I have the task of taking Mary from her grandmother and returning her to her mother. *Great job, thanks.*

We walk into a small interview room at Wellington Central Police Station where Mary is happily sitting on the floor playing with a few toys and drawing pictures. Mary's hair is brushed and tied back neatly. She is wearing probably her best, pretty white Sunday dress. She turns, smiles at us, then returns to her drawing. Also present is a social worker and Mary's grandmother, who I can see is only just holding it together for her granddaughter's sake.

I'm pretty sure the grandmother had prepared Mary the

best she could, but the girl is only young and Grandma is still around, so what does Mary need to worry about? We speak with the social worker and grandmother, getting the details of where Mary is to go.

We listen to the grandmother talk about Mary's life in Fiji, and it sounds idyllic. Mary is obviously loved and cared for. She is clearly a happy wee girl. To say her grandmother is distraught is an understatement. But she respects the law and the court's ruling, so is being as helpful and compliant as possible — despite her grief, loss and agony.

My sergeant and I spend some time playing with Mary, drawing pictures and chatting with her, gaining her trust. The other members of our section are getting ready to finish their shift at 1500 hrs, but we still have a long and very hard afternoon ahead of us.

The moment has come for Grandma to leave and for us to take Mary to meet her mother, who is a total stranger.

Grandma doesn't really know what to do. She isn't crying, but she is shaking uncontrollably. She is battling desperately with her emotions, trying to protect Mary and make this as easy for her as possible — yet Grandma's heart is breaking. She keeps whispering, 'I can't believe this is happening,' even as she smiles at Mary as though everything is normal.

She only gives Mary a hug. I don't think she even says goodbye, but just tells her granddaughter that the nice police ladies are going to look after her. *Yeah right!* Outside the small room I hear Grandma sobbing. It takes all my strength in that moment not to do the same.

We continue to play with Mary as the social worker and Grandma put Mary's few possessions into the boot of our patrol car. It is time for Mary to leave the safety of that room, trust two women she's only just met, and take a ride in a police car.

This wee soul is amazing. So trusting. She knows

Grandma had gone, but that the police officers would look after her. So she feels okay.

The drive takes about half an hour. All the way, my stomach is churning and I am quietly praying there might be an instant bond between mother and daughter, that her new bedroom will be filled with amazing stuff to distract her, and that their reunion will be beautiful to watch.

The suburb we are going to has a few nice houses, lots of okay houses, and lots of run down, unkempt and unloved houses. We pull up outside a house that falls into the third category. We recheck the address. My heart sinks. I look at my sergeant and see she is feeling just the same as me.

Mary's new home is a small, rundown, wooden state house. Paint peeling off worn weatherboards. The lawns haven't been mowed in what looked like years. A car on the grass rusted over last century, and two mongrel dogs roam, rummaging through overflowing rubbish bins.

Home, sweet home.

I look at Mary, immaculately presented, ready to meet her mother. Mary is just staring out the patrol car window. I wonder what she is thinking. I pray she isn't judging her new home as harshly as us.

We lift her small bag of possessions out of the car and make our way through the overgrown weeds. Mary isn't just holding my hand; she keeps a vice-like grip as we navigate our way through the knee-high lawn, keeping a watchful eye on those skinny, roaming dogs.

We reach the open front door and knock. A woman immediately comes to the door. To my relief this is Mum, and she presents well. She bends down to say hello to Mary, who is now cowering behind my legs and hanging on for dear life.

Sadly, no instant recognition. But at least Mum has tried — or so I think until we walk into the house.

She leads us into a room just through the front door

and on the left, saying, 'This is Mary's room.' (*This is Mary's room*. Not speaking to Mary; just making a statement.)

The room is an absolute shambles. It is mid-afternoon and the sun is shining, but not in Mary's room. Rough, tatty curtains are still pulled shut, the bed is unmade. To be truthful, it looks like someone had just climbed out of it. The room is musty and there are toys, or bits and pieces of toys, strewn all over the floor. I am disgusted. *Welcome home, longed-for daughter.*

I turn to talk to Mum, but she's already disappeared.

Another girl has appeared in the doorway of Mary's bedroom. I have no idea who she is or where she lives, but I'll call her 'Angel'. She starts chatting to Mary, picking up toys to show her.

I go in search of Mum, finding her in the lounge where she's talking to a friend on the phone. I make my feelings quite clear: 'Mary needs you right now and she needs one hundred per cent of her mother's attention. We are going and your daughter needs to feel secure. So hang up now!'

She does.

Back in the small dark room I bend down to tell Mary, still standing where I'd left her with Angel and my sergeant, that we are leaving now. Angel keeps up her constant chatter as I explain that we are going and that Mary's mummy will be looking after her now.

Horror and disbelief sweep over her face ... and then the tears start. Tears at first, then sobs from this tiny, vulnerable girl. She hangs onto my leg with strength beyond her years.

Then the worst part. Looking up at me and through wracking sobs, Mary pleads, 'Please, please don't leave me here!'

My sergeant and I are walking out the door, both trying to pry two desperate wee hands off from around my legs.

'Please, police ladies, don't leave me here!'

This is the most tragic, awful moment that breaks my heart, and as I type this, tears are again rolling down my cheeks and my heart physically hurts. Over a decade later, it's still raw.

It feels so wrong to be leaving Mary. *How can I be doing this, something that is technically, in the eyes of the law, right, when it feels like a devastatingly cruel joke?*

Then wee Angel, bless her, steps up. Unlike Mum, who seems to have no idea what to do, Angel says, 'You can come and play with me, I'll show you some cool toys.' She manages to take one of Mary's hands even as the other is still vice-like on my trousers.

I look at Mum, who still doesn't know what to do, and I look at the surroundings.

Taking a deep breath and bending down, I look into Mary's eyes and with a smile and conviction that belies my feelings, firmly but as gently as I can, I remove her small hand and say, 'Mary, you will be okay, you will like it here. This is your mum and she will take good care of you.'

I stand up and repeat this line as I look directly into her mum's eyes.

'Liar!' I am screaming in my head.

We walk out the door, get into the patrol car, don't look back ... and drive off. Now tears are freely flowing down my face.

My sergeant is pretty staunch, but I can see this is just as hard for her as it is for me. 'Are you okay?' she asks.

'No,' I reply, 'but it's done now.'

I was absolutely gutted for Mary and for the role I had played in her journey. It hurt and still does.

Do I think about Mary and how her life has turned out? Oh yes. Yes, I often think about that small, vulnerable girl. But then I have to stop, because if I let my thoughts wander any further I start to feel sick and guilty and start crying again, even all these years later.

I struggled to proofread and 'tidy' this chapter, because every time I read it the words tore at my heart. That's because this is not just a story; this is something that happened to me — and more importantly, something that happened to a little girl through the role I played in her life.

'Mary', if by some miracle you are reading this book and you know this is you, I'd like to apologise.

I'm sorry. I'm so very sorry for that day. For the pain I caused, for the breach of trust you must have felt, for me seemingly taking away any sort of security you had at the time. For changing the course of your young life as you knew it in that moment.

I pray, as I have done for years whenever that day and your face creeps into my thoughts, that you are okay. I pray that you feel loved by those who have been entrusted to love you and take care of you. Because that's what you so deserve.

You are precious and you are loved. You have been created for a purpose and you have a right to feel safe. What happened to you that day was not your fault. It probably felt like you were being punished. You weren't — you did nothing wrong!

This chapter is for all the 'Marys' ... or 'Marks' ... all whose lives may have been ripped apart by other people's choices.

The birth, death and resurrection of Jesus means
that one day everything sad will come untrue ...

— J. R. R. Tolkien

Deepening Desires

I never had to do anything again as heartbreakingly hard as with Mary.

Yes, I saw and dealt with many more tragic situations where vulnerable children and babies were abused and neglected. But I didn't ever feel like I was doing a disservice, a wrong to those I was there to help and protect, as with Mary.

I've always thought: *Why did Mary's mother want her back, when nothing in her behaviour or preparation said that?*

With dear Mary and the role I played in her life, this job hurt the most. Tearing away a little girl's hands from what she thought was a trustworthy and safe person. *Wrong!* That particular job, like no other, wounded my heart, leaving a permanent scar I still feel today.

I wasn't a mother while in the police (probably a good thing, as I may well have kidnapped Mary to look after myself!), but the desire to become one was growing stronger and stronger, and nature wasn't playing its part.

There are some interesting chapters to come on that topic, but I was already starting to realise my desire to have children was shaping the way I dealt with situations at work that involved children.

I am on duty and working alone one day when I am dispatched to a job at an abortion clinic. My role is to ask a vocal protestor to move on as he is blocking the path and making it difficult and stressful for a woman who is trying to enter the clinic.

Torn. On the one hand, here is a woman who is obviously pregnant and for whatever reason is trying to enter the clinic to have an abortion.

Another backstory I don't know, so I'm not to judge. *Compassion. No stones.* This is hard for me. Hard not for me to well up and be unprofessional and say to her, 'You may not want to have the baby that is growing within you, for whatever reason, but I desperately want you to have that baby.'

I want to tell her that I'm not falling pregnant and am struggling with that reality. I want to tell her how it breaks my heart but also gives me great joy whenever friends tell me they can fall pregnant by just looking at their partners. I desperately want what she and they have! The longing, as I looked at her belly, is so overwhelmingly powerful and desperate.

On the other hand — my police hand — is the protestor. Saying all the things I feel: 'Life is precious, there is a baby growing inside you, you're its mother. It doesn't get a say in this, it trusts you to protect it.' (*Just like Mary!* I think.)

But with my police hat on, emotions tightly compartmentalised and squashed down within me, I professionally and authoritatively go and speak with the protestor. I explain this woman has a right to enter the building. 'Yes, what she is doing might go against everything you believe in, but it is her body and her right and you don't know anything about her circumstances. So be passionate, but be compassionate too.'

I carefully help the woman out of the car where she has

been 'hiding'. I feel sad that she is by herself at this time. My arm around her, I walk her past the now silent protestor and into the clinic. She tearfully thanks me. I don't know what to say, so I give her a long hug.

The protestor glares at me as I leave. He's not shouting anymore, he doesn't need to. The billboard he is frantically waving and the look on his face speak volumes.

I understand his heart. But I am learning that sometimes we need to drop our stones and walk away. Find a way to proclaim our message with love and respect, rather than with a hate that knows and cares nothing for a person's backstory.

This is a really hard topic. I see the argument, the dilemma and the rationalisation from both sides.

I have a dear friend who is a midwife. She is a great storyteller and I often have a huge belly laugh when I hear some of the things she has seen and dealt with while delivering babies. However, I remember one day when she was upset and shaken by something that had happened during one of her hospital shifts, two days before Mother's Day.

She had been tasked to look after a woman who had been in J Ward, but had to be shifted into the maternity ward, as beds in J Ward were needed by others. J Ward is where abortions are carried out.

My friend is told there is a woman in her thirties, nineteen weeks pregnant, who doesn't want the baby and has already been given medication to induce the birth. Her husband is with her. You just need to monitor her and deliver the baby when it comes.

Being given medication to induce the baby doesn't kill the baby in the womb; it just makes the woman go into early labour, tricking the body that it's time to deliver. So the body sets about doing what it's supposed to, even though it's weeks too early. This is almost too much for my friend and she prays her shift will finish before the baby is born.

Before going in to see the woman she reads her file. She discovers, among other things, that the reason the woman has decided to get an abortion now is because her career has already suffered from the birth of her first baby and she can't cope with having another baby at this time.

Determined to keep her own emotions in check, my friend goes in to see how the woman is doing. It has been about ten hours since the woman was given her medication.

'How are you doing?'

'It's been ten hours now. Why isn't this working? It's still moving inside me. I can feel it.'

My friend bites her tongue. *I can feel it.*

At this age the baby is about fourteen to sixteen centimetres long. The gender of the baby is known, the heart's been busy pumping blood around the body and up to the brain for a long time. Baby has eyelids, eyebrows and fingernails. I'm not a doctor, but the list could go on.

Without going into too much more detail the day progresses but the baby, obviously putting up a good fight, is not about to come out. The woman starts telling my friend and her husband she is too tired now and doesn't want any more drugs; she just wants to go home.

My friend has to ask: 'You're telling me now you want to keep your baby and you want to go home?'

'I'm just tired and want to go home.'

My friend's shift ends before any decision is made.

The next day there is no sign of the woman and my friend asks after her. She's told the woman later went home, still pregnant and had rung the next morning asking to be referred to a midwife to help see her through the next twenty weeks of her pregnancy. She was keeping her baby.

I don't know what happened after that. I don't know the

woman's name, of course. But I used to briefly flick my eyes over the birth announcements in the paper wondering which little baby was the one nearly was not wanted. Would that baby know? Would his or her parents tell them in the future what they nearly did? Would their baby feel loved?

At the time, my friend told me that if babies are born premature, from twenty-three weeks the doctors and nurses try to save them. But from twenty weeks, if a little baby is born, it will try to breathe on its own. It will struggle as its lungs aren't fully developed. But it will try.

Watching a documentary about terrible atrocities that happened in Zimbabwe, I learnt that one of the weapons of war used against women and girls is rape. A vicious, terrible thing. Yet the next thing I saw in this documentary was a classroom of women, girls really, learning English and other subjects. Most of them holding babies. All the babies conceived out of rape by soldiers.

One mother explained, 'I have called my baby "Hope" as, despite how she was conceived, it is not her fault and she brings me hope for my future. I love her.'

Every person puts a different value on life.

In the year ended 2014, according to Statistics New Zealand, 13,137 abortions were performed in New Zealand. This was the lowest number since 1994's total of 12,835. That is 14.4 abortions per 1000 women aged between 15 and 44.

Again this is really hard to write about, but Mary's story, my work in the police, that of my midwife friend, and my own journey of trying to have children have become a huge part of my who I am. So many emotions battle within me when I think about this topic.

I can't help but relate little Mary, hanging onto what she saw as a trustworthy person, to a vulnerable baby inside its mum. *Trusting.* The adult is there to protect.

I read a newspaper article reporting that Down Syndrome

could become a rare disorder because of safer prenatal tests. 'Though blood-based tests would become far more prominent,' a professor said, 'it was important screening guidelines emphasised women had a choice, whether or not they had the tests.'

The article continued: 'Prenatal tests, opposed by Down Syndrome advocates, were not a "slippery slope" to Third Reich genocidal acts, nor were they an indication the syndrome was considered a "best-avoided disease". For some families, raising a DS child will be immensely difficult, and so by offering termination we conceded that a DS child will be seen as being too great a burden for some.'

The following week, March 2013, I read an article from *Next Magazine*: 'My partner Jessi and I have a son who has an extra chromosome in each one of his cells, he has Down's Syndrome. He is five years old. His name is Stetson Blue and he is a blessing who arrived in a very clever disguise. Don't get me wrong. Being a mother of a special needs child has plenty of tough moments. But I've learnt a few things from our son, the central lesson being that having a child who is "different" is one of the most profound experiences a parent can have because it cuts to what is, for me, the very essence of life. We weren't put on this earth to be perfect. We are here to give. We are here to grow in compassion. We are here to learn how to love, absolutely and freely.

'After all, do we have children in our desire to complete and perfect our lives, or do we have children so we can love them unconditionally (and that includes loving all the crazy obstacles that come with them)? I had a choice. I could decide to see our little boy as something deficient ... or I could see him as a chance to love not in spite of, but because.'

One message from society says that raising a Down Syndrome child is too hard a burden to bear. It sits alongside another from a mother who calls her Down Syndrome son a blessing.

Then, another article in *Next Magazine*, from January 2016. Written bravely and so honestly from a mother who had an abortion. Her reasons? 'The father of this unborn child was in my life (and still is), but already had grown-up children and had never professed any desire to have another family. Apart from anything else, I felt I was just too bloody old and I was angry. I was angry with myself, with the foetus, with whichever part of me had been so negligent and landed me in this position.'

She goes on: 'The night before my appointment I lay in bed and I stopped feeling angry.... I put my hand on my (fat) tummy and said goodbye to my beautiful, unborn child. I said I loved them. I said I was sorry but I could not keep them. I cried soft, sad tears .... Years later, I still think I did (the right thing), although I remember my unborn child and the age they would be.'

Each of us has different opinions and values. We have all walked different paths to be where we are today. We all think we are right and can fully justify what and why we think as we do. (I know I do!) But I have to keep reminding myself, when my judgemental thoughts come to the fore, that until I've been in an incredibly difficult situation, whatever it may be, how can I ever judge someone for what they do and decisions they make? It's not my place to judge.

Don't get me wrong, I've challenged friends when I feel decisions and paths they are taking are very wrong. I don't think abortions are right, just let me say that. (I'm picking you will have understood that from what I've said.) However — and there must be a 'however' — I would not and will not ever judge a woman who has gone through the trauma of an abortion for whatever reason. I've never walked in that person's shoes.

Jesus didn't judge. (Remember that story?) It's easy to judge others when they sin differently than you. I'm learning to put my stone down.

I do believe it breaks God's heart every time one of his most vulnerable creations is taken too soon. God sheds heartbroken tears, but also compassionate tears for the mother.

For those of you reading this who have had an abortion for whatever reason, please do not feel I've said these words to judge you. As I keep reiterating, these are stories that make up my life and have moulded me, my beliefs and my personality.

As you read this, you may still feel pain or guilt. Maybe you feel relief. Maybe you have carried a secret like this for too long and it needs to be shared. Do what you need to.

But I would suggest Jesus. My opinion, based on my experiences, is that he will bring comfort and, if you ask, forgiveness. I do believe this is something that Jesus died on the cross for. A price must be paid for the death of a child, no matter whether the law says it is okay or not. It has cost the child everything and, in different ways, it costs the mother too, for life.

In the meantime, I believe God in Heaven is protecting your child, and one day they will be gladly waiting to meet you.

My clever brother is a gifted musician, singer and songwriter. He penned a song, originally inspired by the brutal beating to death of a New Zealand toddler by his parents (a tragedy that has become all too frequent these days). The song, called 'Beautiful Child', off Craig's album *Surrender*, gives hope.

With his permission I quote the lyrics:

Beautiful child gone before your life had begun,
taken away from her womb,
what has she done,
but now your spirit is soaring.

You're with Jesus now,
as you run and play through Heaven's open doors,
you know He will take care of you,
you're with Jesus now,
as He turns and looks into your longing eyes,
and tells you that He loves you child.

When your world is torn apart before your eyes,
your beautiful child is taken away all too soon,
but now their spirit is soaring,

So don't be afraid,
you're here with me now, you'll see your loved ones again,
I'll show you her face,
you see she's hurting,
but you're here to welcome her in,
my beautiful child,
there's so much to see,
so come with me now through all eternity,
and feel your spirit soaring.

As you run and play through Heaven's open doors,
you know He will take care of you,
you're with Jesus now
as He turns and looks into your longing eyes,
and tells you that He loves you child,
you're with Jesus now,
you're home now,
you're home now,
you're home now.

To hear Craig singing this song, go to
www.craigmckenzie.nz.

Celebrating Mum's 21st. Birthday girl in the middle with proud fiancé by her side. (Photo: Douglas Probert)

Mum and Dad's wedding day, 3 February 1968. Surrounded by immediate family. (Photo: Simon Woolf Snr)

Cadets training to be Officers of The Salvation Army. Craig is in the photo — he just hasn't 'arrived' yet. (Photo: Alan Robb)

Salvation Army girls in winter uniform. In action with timbrels, tenor horn and cornet. Sheryn, third from left. (Photo: Craig McKenzie)

Summer uniform and big late '80s hair! Sheryn,
far right. (Photo: Craig McKenzie)

Graduation day, 14 February 1992. Yes, Sheryn is the shortest
new constable in the front row. (Photo: Craig McKenzie)

Celebrating the dream with family. (Photo: Andrea Jackson)

The Adamson family. From the left, Brad, Mark (on floor),
Jane, Kaye, Warner and Kathryne. (Photo: Sheryn Adamson)

Wedding day, 11 September 1993. (Photo: Simon Woolf Jnr)

Happy newly-wed constables. Both sporting
'90s hair! (Photo: Mel McKenzie)

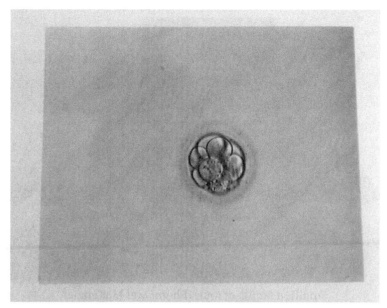

Tayla's embryo. Three days old in her petri
dish. (Photo: Fertility Associates)

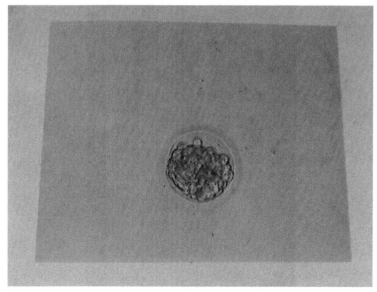

Rylee's blastocyst. Six days old in her petri
dish. (Photo: Fertility Associates)

Finally, a family of four. (Photo: Mel McKenzie)

Two beautiful girls. (Photo: Sheryn Adamson)

The journey continues. Celebrating Dad's 70th birthday. (Photo: Shelley Probert)

The true measure of a man is not how he behaves
in moments of comfort and convenience but how
he stands at times of controversy and challenges.

— Martin Luther King Jr.

How To Make Babies

I hold the needle about five centimetres from my bare skin. My hand isn't shaking, but I am nervous. It's my first time and I don't know if I can do this or what it will feel like. Tears start to well in my eyes and my vision begins to blur. I move the needle away and look at my husband sitting next to me.

'You can do it,' Brad says. 'It won't hurt, you're brave.'

I say, 'I'm not worried about the pain — this is just not how you're supposed to make babies.'

It's 6:45 am, we've both stumbled out of bed, we're in our dressing gowns and sitting on the couch. I am about to inject myself in the stomach as we start the scary, emotional and unknown journey into the world of In Vitro Fertilisation (IVF) treatment. The hopeful desired outcome? A baby or two. The procedure? Not how God originally intended babies to be conceived.

I'm not feeling attractive or turned on, but I am hoping this still intimate moment will produce a child. It may in the long run, but I also know a lot of medication, stress, tears and people have to be involved in the process yet.

Our infertility journey began seven years before this day. I'd always known my husband had experienced a severe case of mumps when he was sixteen. At the time, his doctor told him he now had only a fifty-fifty chance of fathering a child. A rugby playing, sixteen-year-old boy, worried or thinking about being a father? *She'll be right, Doc!*

Even when Brad first told me this when we were seeing each other and then going on to get married, having children was the furthest thing from my mind too. Yes, I wanted kids, but much, much later. I was just loving my career.

Six years into our marriage I came off the contraceptive pill because there was a scare at the time that it could be linked to blood clots. But after coming to this decision, month after month my periods got more and more painful.

While Brad and I were in Nelson for a friend's wedding and a romantic weekend away together, my body decided to play havoc. I woke at 5 am with crippling pain in my abdomen and couldn't get back to sleep. I told Brad to go for a run and leave me alone. I didn't want him to be around me. (I'm a bit like an animal when sick. I just want to be by myself, heal and eventually re-emerge from my cave when well. I don't like the feeling of being 'weak'.)

I ended up on the floor and was on the verge of fainting. I was vomiting and experiencing pain in my lower abdomen like I'd never felt before.

While lying in the foetal position I truly thought I was going to die. I didn't relate my pain or what I was experiencing to a monthly period.

When Brad returned from his run, he wanted to take me straight to the hospital, but being my usual stubborn self, I refused, promising instead to see our doctor once back in Wellington.

Back home, keeping my promise and seeing my doctor, she promptly told me I might have endometriosis and referred me to a specialist. (Google 'endometriosis' for a full rundown — this book is not about periods and the like! But do appreciate that endometriosis is a crippling disease and if your periods or that of your daughters are extremely painful, you should check out the symptoms and chat to your GP.)

Endometriosis, which I'd only heard of because a friend had suffered from it and it had affected her ability to have children, became 'affectionately' known to me as 'endo'. My fabulous specialist said she'd like to do laparoscopic surgery to see what was going on. If she found any endo or other 'bad stuff' she would get rid of it.

'Fine,' I said. 'How long will that take?'

'Should be around an hour or so, maybe up to three hours at the most, and you'll be either home that day or the next.'

After a five-hour operation and two days in hospital, my specialist confirmed that yes, I had endometriosis. Absolutely riddled with it, she explained. Cysts on my ovaries the size of golf balls, organs stuck together that shouldn't have been stuck. 'Your insides look very, very angry. You were a mess, Sheryn.'

With that comment, I realised what I had been doing. All those years of tiring shift work, thriving on adrenaline highs, but also squashing down the anger, frustration, fear, injustice, pain and sadness in my day-to-day life as a police officer. My body had consumed all of this physically and that was now being revealed. Life had taken a toll.

'Great! It's gone and I'm better, yes?' I optimistically said to my doctor.

'No, Sheryn, things need to change.'

Again, without going into all the details of endo, there is no one-off, one hundred per cent cure. For me, it was about making some major lifestyle changes. Brad and I were also told by the specialist that if we wanted to have a family, we should get down to business ASAP. After explaining about the mumps Brad had at sixteen, Brad, lucky guy, was off for his own set of fun tests.

And so, with all our medical results and information in hand, we went to our first appointment with the IVF specialists.

Feeling nervous doesn't even come close to describing how I felt. I was so conscious of what my gynaecologist had said after seeing our test results. 'The only way you're going to possibly have a family is by doing IVF!'

I walk into the Fertility Associates' building feeling so self-conscious. I have only told a few really close friends about all the stuff we are going through trying to start a family, but I haven't told a soul — other than my parents and brother — that we are looking into IVF. I don't want to be spotted walking into this building.

The waiting room is quiet. Gentle background music plays on a radio somewhere. I am hoping I don't see anyone else I know. Couples sit huddled together on couches, all of us grabbing sly glances at each other. As I look at the other 'normal' couples around me, it brings home the fact that so many others are going through exactly what we are experiencing.

I want to hide the 'infertile couple' label that I feel is plastered across my forehead, but somehow it just sticks there. I don't like being here because it means I'm not in control of what my body is doing and I that need help.

I know this feeling and experience happens every day in waiting rooms all over the world. People waiting for a diagnosis. One sentence from the doctor: *benign, malignant, more tests required, I'm sorry*. Life frustratingly out of our control.

After a while, a smartly-dressed, distinguished-looking doctor introduces himself. We are invited into his office.

Sitting in the room is a twenty-something attractive woman. We are told she's in training to be a doctor and will be sitting in on our consultation, if that's okay with us? What else do we say but 'great'? *That's fine, we'll chat about some of our most intimate stuff and I'll probably cry because it's such an emotional thing to be discussing. But fine, let the young lady stay — let's invite a few others in case I feel the need for a group hug.*

'Yes, that's okay.' I'm too polite, too on edge and too nervous to say otherwise.

Over the next little while, the doctor explains that after looking through our medical files and talking to us he has come to a helpful conclusion. Which is: even if I was one hundred per cent okay, we still couldn't have kids because of Brad's sperm count, the result of his teenage mumps. The helpful doctor goes on to explain some more: even if Brad was one hundred per cent, we still couldn't have kids because of the severity of my endo.

His concluding statement hangs in the air: 'You couldn't have ended up with more incompatible partners — the chances of you two conceiving, even with IVF, are less than ten per cent.'

This day was just getting better all the time.

But wait, there's more. Next he says, 'But while you are here we might as well examine you (that's lucky me, not Brad). Just pop next door, remove the bottom half of your clothing and put the sheet over yourself.'

Lying on the bed, having done what was asked of me, I try to relax the best I can. The lights are dim and I'm feeling reasonably comfortable when the doctor walks in, followed by his young trainee. *Great, show time!*

I'm lying there with a mantra running through my mind: *Relax, relax, relax.*

'Okay, just bring your heels up together and let your knees drop open.'

I obey. *Relax, relax, relax.*

Doctor and trainee then have the following discussion …

Doctor: 'Right, you can put the scapular clamp in place.'

Trainee: 'No, I'd prefer you to do it and I'll watch.'

'No, you can do it; it will be good for you.'

'No, I really don't want to.'

'Come on, you'll be fine.'

'No, I'll do it next time. Okay?'

Hello, what about me?! Do I get a say in the matter? Oh no, I'll just lie here naked from the waist down, legs open and with a spotlight shining on me while you two argue!

Finally, after some more toing and froing, the doctor finally relents and without another word, does the entire procedure himself. It takes every bit of strength I have to keep from crying.

My head is a mess. I feel so humiliated, so stripped of my dignity. I am hating every minute of this. I want to get up and run out. The only thing keeping me on that bed, apart from the fact I have no pants on and a scapular clamp coldly inserted, is the very faint thought *(hope!)* that this is our way of making babies.

Finally I'm back sitting next to Brad, fully clothed and with my happy face on. I know my face is pale and the inside of my lips are almost bleeding because I'm biting them hard so I don't cry. The doctor then explains, in full detail, the whole IVF procedure, which is actually really quite helpful and informative.

'Now, do you have any other questions?'

'Yes, lots!'

The plan is to get me to inject myself with different drugs that will cause my body to produce more than just the usual one to two eggs, hopefully twelve or so. My eggs will then be removed and injected with sperm (if Brad was able to produce enough 'live, good quality' ones). And then they will select the best fertilised eggs to replace in me at the right time.

Question: 'So ... what happens if we do end up with twelve embryos (fertilised eggs) and have the couple of children we are hoping for? What happens with the spare ones?'

'We either discard them, or you can take them home and do that. Or you could donate them.'

'Okay, so here's our moral issue and what we'd like to do. We would prefer to only fertilise, say, four eggs. And if we end up with four kids, great, but at least there will be no "leftovers" to dilemma over. Because for us, once an egg is fertilised, we see it has the potential to become a baby and we would feel we at least need to give it that chance.'

'Yes, that's true,' says the doctor, 'but it hardly ever works out that all the eggs we inject sperm into turn into embryos, and not all embryos when replaced will work, so we like you to create as many as possible to give you and us the best chance.'

'We understand that, but for us to do IVF, we have this moral issue and so we don't want to fertilise twelve eggs. Is that possible?'

'No, it's not really. Sometimes you just have to get over your morals to get what you want.'

Another statement that just hangs in the air.

I couldn't believe he just said that, because for me that was it. This doctor, with that one statement, had shut the door on IVF for us. Because I was not going to 'get over my morals to get what I want'. As much as 'I wanted'.

What I did want, right then, was to get out of that room. In fact, I can't remember any more of our conversation after that statement.

Brad and I silently leave the building, holding hands and walking into the bright sunlight. I feel degraded and as if all my hope had been stripped from me. I burst out crying. All my pent-up emotions flow out. *Gutted. Humiliated. Heartbroken.*

We talk on the way home, both knowing the door has just been shut on us doing IVF. And for the next few years I experience roller coaster after roller coaster of emotions.

We were officially an infertile couple. We couldn't have children; we were different. That choice had been taken from us — and that's what hurt and felt the hardest, having no control. Control, part of my make-up, take it away from me and it hits and hurts me hard.

I had been telling people we weren't ready to have kids yet because everyone asked all the time: 'Isn't it about time you had kids?' 'How long have you been married now? You'd better have a family soon, hadn't you?' 'Your body clock must be ticking?'

Every question was a knife wound into my already broken heart. Screaming inside, 'You've no idea how I feel!' Yet I continued to put on my happy face and kept on replying, 'We're not really big on kids — we'll think about it one day.' *Self-protection.* I was embarrassed and ashamed to be infertile.

I finally reached emotional breaking point and simply could not pull out my happy face any more. So, one Sunday in a church service, we told people the whole sad story. I got Brad to read out what I had written as there was no way I would have been able to get through it.

There it was, out there, no more questions, no more pressure. *Just everyone back off and leave me alone with my lack of control and pain!*

Except for one question: *why?* Three letters in a huge, frustrating word. A word often not answered to anyone's satisfaction. *Why that child? Why that friend or family member? Why me? Why not me? What have I done?*

All the police jobs I'd attended where babies and children were so badly treated. 'Just give me a chance,' I'd cry, 'I'll be a good mum.' Mary would pop into my head. I would have looked after her. Those times I'd attended abortion clinics and the sad longing I felt inside. My midwife friend's story. Stories I'd read in magazines.

I wanted a baby! I wanted to be a mum. I would take such good care of our child.

I wanted what I couldn't have. And I wanted what others had. I was angry, frustrated, broken and — above all else — desperately sad.

Yesterday is gone. Tomorrow has not yet come. We have only today. Let us begin.

— Mother Teresa

Seven Years

About four years after saying no to IVF, knowing it was not right for us to do it in the way that was being offered, we were still praying and believing for our miracle baby. Yet God was not giving us what we wanted.

Did I sometimes get angry at God? Yes, of course. As a Christian, my relationship with God is like that of a child dearly loved by a good father. What child doesn't get angry and frustrated with a parent who won't give them whatever they want and whenever they want it?

But did this stop me believing in God? No. For me, that would be like not believing in my earthly dad because he doesn't give me what I want when I want it. Despite my feelings and frustrations, it doesn't change the fact that my dad is still there and very real. So no, this didn't cause me to doubt God's existence.

On my journey I've learnt that God does answer my prayers, usually in one of three ways: yes, no or wait.

There were times when I would be at peace and able to trust that my future, whatever it may look like, would be perfect for me, and I would be okay with that. If I wasn't going to be a mother in the physical sense then, I could live with that. But I still had hope.

I attended meetings where lots of people prayed for God to heal Brad and me. I had good days when I could cope with my emotions. I had bad days. And I had terrible days. I was still putting on a happy face when surrounded by pregnant women and babies and happy families, although I would often make excuses not to go to children's birthday parties, baby showers, Mother's Days and children's Sundays at church. It hurt too much.

Every month I'd be thinking, 'Is this it?' Only to have my hopes dashed. I would go through those patches and say, 'Alright God, if it's not your will for us to have kids, I'm okay with that.' Then the next day totally reneging on that and begging God, 'Please, let me have a baby!' An inbuilt rollercoaster that I really wanted to get off.

Then this happened ...

You could call it random, but I don't believe it was. I cleared the letterbox to find a newsletter from the Fertility Associates clinic. In the early stages of our journey we used to receive stuff from them all the time, but it stopped after a few years. So this seemed quite out of the blue. When I opened it, what it said stopped me in my tracks.

The newsletter basically said: 'Technology is getting better all the time, we know people have had 'issues' with creating a copious amount of embryos and wondering what to do with the "leftovers", so if this is you please come back and see us as we'd like to talk again.'

Hope welled up again, along with tears and a little bit of scepticism.

Brad and I prayed, saying to God something along the lines of: 'If we are not supposed to do IVF, make that absolutely clear to us and keep the doors firmly shut, or else give us a real peace about the way ahead.'

We made an appointment with Fertility Associates, and seeing a different doctor this time, once again entered the IVF world.

After about a half-an-hour discussion with our new doctor (no trainee in tow), it was incredibly clear that all the 'moral issues' we'd previously had no longer stood in our way. We explained what we had been told last time, only wanting to fertilise four eggs but being told to get over our morals.

The doctor said, 'Well, technically you can now do that, but you really are limiting your chances. However, if that's what you want to do then that's your choice — and we can go ahead and do it.' I was trying not to let hope burst out of my chest, but I wanted to dash across the room and kiss this doctor.

I looked at Brad and knew he was thinking the same as me (not the kissing part, but that the doors seemed to be flying open for us). That seed of hope was well and truly watered and a wee shoot had burst out of our dark sadness.

After much more discussion and prayer we decided to go ahead with the procedure. Also, after more debate with the doctor, we were a little persuaded/reasoned into fertilizing six eggs, not four. We figured, 'Well, life would never be the same again, but if God wants us to end up with six kids then so be it!'

At every step of the IVF journey I was continually praying, 'Please God, if this is wrong or if we are supposed to keep waiting and not do IVF, then please, please close the doors and make it clear we should stop.' But God never did close those doors.

Every step went absolutely perfectly. No hiccups, no problems. Yes, it was emotional. Yes, it was scary and draining and physically challenging. But it was okay.

As an aside to this IVF journey, Brad was going through a particularly stressful time at work. For a lot of the time while

I was injecting myself he was out of town, but on the days and for the appointments he needed to be at, it just seemed to work out that Brad could make it.

During one particular stage, I had to join Brad in another city and because of the delicate nature of the IVF injections, which have to be administered at exactly the same time each day, I had to take my injections on the plane trip, injecting myself in the tiny bathroom. All part of making babies for Brad and me.

On the day they took my eggs out, twelve healthy eggs were removed. The embryologist confirmed that we only wanted six of these fertilised. We said yes, even after we were told we had less than ten per cent chance of any of them working.

One other point to note, when Brad had to produce his all-important 'sample', out of the millions of live sperm most men have, Brad had just six sperm suitable to be used. *Random coincidence? I think not.* Six!

Once I left the theatre after having my eggs removed, Brad again had to leave Wellington to catch a plane to another city. This was hard, but I knew there was nothing he could do now. I stayed with my parents that night. I vividly remember thinking as I tried to go to sleep that tomorrow the embryologist will phone and say if any of the eggs have fertilised. Surreal and also sad, knowing Brad would have to be waiting to hear the news in another city.

The phone rings the next morning at 8:30 am sharp and suddenly all conversation in our house stops. I take a deep breath and answer. Because of the sensitive nature of IVF the embryologist asks,

'Is this Sheryn Adamson?'

'Yes.'

'Are you in a position to speak now about your embryos?'

'Yes.'

'Congratulations, all six eggs have fertilised and are growing.'

Oh-kaaay! From none to six.

Excited, relieved, overwhelmed, but trying not to get too hopeful, as there is still a long way to go. Oh yes, and tears.

The lady says, 'I'll call you again tomorrow to report on their progress.'

I hang up the phone, look at Mum, Dad and my brother ... and announce: 'Well, at this stage we potentially have six children!'

After hugs and more tears I call Brad.

I give him the same 'potential six kids' message. After a short silence, his typical 'you're joking!' disbelief is verbalised, albeit happily.

The next day the reality of the IVF procedure starts to hit home as the embryologist rings to say two of our embryos have stopped developing and there are only four left. This is what the doctors, both of them, warned us about.

I guess there's a hint of relief, but also sadness at losing two embryos, even though this is totally normal and can happen to any woman, whether doing IVF or not. Usually women don't even know when an embryo has been created. But I do feel sad. Our tiny, life-multiplying embryos were literally out in the open, every step of their development and growth on display.

The third day is the big one, the day of replacement. Provided there are still viable embryos to use.

The embryologist calls again, Saturday morning, with the hopeful news all four little embryos are still growing. Three are exactly right in their developmental stage — one is lagging a bit, but it is still alright. It is confirmed that we will definitely be having an embryo replaced that morning.

I ring Brad with the great news. He's still away. Not even in the same city as me, so we won't be together on this very important, long awaited day. It feels weird that he isn't going to be with me when I get pregnant. (Yes, weird!) My parents will be in the room with me though. (Another interesting concept: husband absent, but parents present while making babies!)

I don't remember being scared-nervous; it was more an excited-nervous. Hopeful. (Yes, that tender wee shoot of hope was still growing.)

The procedure went incredibly smoothly. Totally painless.

A few funny moments when the lovely doctor replacing the embryo realised my dad was actually 'my dad' and not my 'quite a bit older than me' husband. The doctor looked quite relieved when I laughed and confirmed that this was, in fact, my father!

It was an amazing experience watching the embryologist hand the doctor a long thin tube that contained our embryo, and then watching a monitor to see the embryo put inside me. It was all over in fifteen minutes. Mum, Dad and I went and had a coffee together, and for the first time in our journey of infertility I could consider myself technically pregnant, even though Brad hadn't been present!

The next two weeks of waiting just about did my head in emotionally. Knowing there was nothing I could do but wait. Again, frustration at my lack of control.

As the day of my blood test that would confirm whether or not I was pregnant drew nearer, I dreaded going to the toilet in case there were signs my period was coming. I wondered what every little feeling, every little tweak in my stomach meant. Good sign or bad?

The day of my blood test was a busy one at work. I knew I had to go out that night as well, and as Brad was away till the next day I decided not to get my results till the following morning when Brad would be coming home.

On arriving at work after my blood test, I encountered

a dear friend of mine who had obviously been crying — yet she was smiling at me. She came into my office and began saying things like, 'You are a blessed woman. God is blessing you; you are going to have a baby.' I was stunned. This friend knew of our infertility, but not one person other than my parents and brother knew we had being doing IVF. I had been working with this woman for about two years and she'd never said anything like this, but she just felt God had laid this on her heart that morning. I broke down and told her about the blood test I'd just been for. It was an amazing emotional time together.

A couple of months before this, another friend who knew only a little of our journey rang me at work. She said, 'I don't usually do this, but I really feel God has given me a verse from the bible for you. I can't get you or the verse out of my head, so I have to share it with you. It's from Psalm 113:9 (TLB) and says: *He (God) gives children to the childless wife, so that she becomes a happy mother. Hallelujah, Praise the Lord.*

The 8th of September 2005. I'm alone at home. Brad is arriving in Wellington around lunchtime when I will pick him up from work at the Wellington Central Police Station and tell him our news.

I wake in the morning feeling surprisingly at peace. I have no great feeling about whether I'm pregnant or not. All I know is I feel at peace and that at 8:30 am I can ring the fertility clinic and get my results.

At 8:30 am, on the dot, I'm sitting alone at our breakfast bar dialling the number. The receptionist answers and I'm put through to the nurse.

'Hi, it's Sheryn Adamson and I'm ringing for my pregnancy results.'

'Okay, just a minute please.'

I'm put on hold and listen to some elevator music. This

is surreal. I've been waiting seven years for this moment and I'm listening to elevator music.

'Sheryn Adamson?'

'Yes.'

'Congratulations, you're pregnant.'

Waves of relief, disbelief, shock, hope — everything! — flood over me. I feel hot fat tears pouring down my cheeks.

'I think I'm a little in shock, I'm not sure if I can talk.'

'It's okay to cry, dear. Do you want me to call you back?'

'No, no,' I manage to say. 'Just tell me what you said again?'

She laughs. 'Congratulations Sheryn, you're going to have a baby.'

After instructions about more monitoring blood tests, I finally hang up and just sit on my couch for I don't know how long. Thanking God, crying, laughing, and holding my flat stomach. Still not really believing, but that tiny shoot called hope has just shot through the roof with my blood test results.

I still have three hours to wait before I can see and tell Brad. I go for a long walk and hope people aren't too concerned when they see a laughing, crying woman out walking. I rehearse in my mind how and what I'm going to say to Brad. To be truthful, I have actually been doing this for years, rehearsing these lines, but this time it's for real.

Lunchtime. I'm sitting in our car, waiting outside the police station, watching for Brad. I don't want him to see my face till I'm ready to tell him as he can read me like a book and I want to tell him myself.

I see him coming out the door so I quickly get out of the car and stand at the back of the vehicle. He's looking at me. I don't think he can tell. I start crying as he stands in front of me and holds me. 'We are having a baby!' I blurt out. I don't really say it how I wanted to or had practised — I don't think

I even smiled. Just those five words mixed with now copious amounts of tears, snot and sobbing.

What a moment!

Seven long years of grief, pain and held-onto hope is being allowed to flow out, and I just cry. The relief.

The next hour is amazing. I recount the whole morning and telephone conversation to Brad.

We go and meet my brother and share more tears and hugs. Then off to see my dad who's at work. We hug for a long time (and cry, funny that!) when I tell him he's going to be a grandfather. Mum is in London, so the tears and telling her have to wait a few days.

When she arrives home, we are all waiting at the airport. I see her walking up the concourse to where we have been standing and I hold up a sign I've made. It says, 'Welcome home Grandma.' More tears.

I could recount moment after moment of special times telling people. To tell friends who had journeyed with us over the past seven years was just amazing. Going into baby shops, buying *our* baby's first pieces of clothing. Euphoric joy.

Best. Time. Ever.

I still had (and have) questions though.

Why did it take seven years of so much pain, heartache and waiting? Why did we have to do IVF when I totally believed, and still do, that God could have allowed me to become pregnant without medical intervention? Why do some people do IVF for years and it never works? Why do some end up having babies only for them to die tragically young? Why do some people keep having kids when they don't seem to really want them, or can't look after them as they deserve, or end up abusing them? Why are abortion rates so high? Why?!

So many whys that I don't know the answers to. Lots of my why questions to God still remain unanswered and I have to accept this. That's faith. (Hence our daughter's middle name.) 'Now faith is being sure of what we hope for and certain of what we do not see.' (Hebrews 11:1, NIV)

For now, though, I was pregnant. *Finally.*

It's ok to be a glowstick; sometimes we need to break before we shine.

— Anon

Breaking Point

Let me just back up a bit and talk about the 'during' of our seven years. There were happy times when I'd manage to switch off or put out of my head the fact that we were different.

I managed to go to hospital room after hospital room to congratulate, oooh and ahhh over friends' babies ... baby after baby after baby. Still with a bit of self-protection, though — I would often buy gifts for the parents, not something for the new baby. I'd say, 'You guys deserve a treat too.' I just didn't want to go into any baby shops or risk being seen in one. Too much pain and too many questions.

Then things started to change.

I started to hide away from people, not wanting to go to events or parties since I'd have to talk to people and they might ask personal questions. I retreated further and further into myself, preferring only to hang out with my closest family members since I knew I was safe with them.

I ended up taking three months off work to try and sort myself out. I really couldn't cope with life and people anymore.

One particular day I was sitting outside. I was on a deck

chair, the sun was at a perfect temperature and there was a gentle breeze. I was looking at my house trying to make the effort to bring to mind how blessed I was to have such an amazing husband, an amazing family and to live in a lovely home — yet I'd never felt so sad and depressed. Tears streamed down my face.

I said to God, through fountains of tears, 'It's too hard! You've got to do something today to ease this pain. It's too much for me to bear.'

I decided I had to phone Mum, who was living in Perth, Western Australia, at the time. I had no idea what time it was over there, and I was in no state to figure it out. I phoned her at home on a workday, but she just 'happened' to be there when I rang. I don't know how long I spent crying on the phone to Mum, getting out words that wouldn't have made any sense because a high, garbled, sobbing voice doesn't work properly when you're crying. Dear Mum, just listening, agreeing, crying and praying with me. Then, as I was hanging up, the doorbell went.

At my front door was a courier.

It was surprising I even opened the door because I had got to the point where I wouldn't usually answer the phone or door anymore. I wanted to stay hidden.

That same courier ended up knocking at my door twice that day with two fabulous bunches of flowers from two separate people. These people would have had no idea what a bad day I was having.

The courier even made the comment (since my tear-streaked face would have been a dead giveaway that I was in the middle of a very bad day) that I must really be needing these flowers. Guys reading this chapter might not get how huge that was, but for a woman, two beautiful bunches of flowers in one day; well, it truly got me through my lowest day.

For me, this was a practical and tangible way I knew God

was pouring out his love for me. Yes, again you could say it was just a coincidence. You could say it was from the 'universe'. But Brad and I had told no one about our journey. My parents and brother only — that was it. These flowers came from a friend living overseas and a person in Wellington.

So for me, God, my Heavenly Father, knowing how his child was feeling, brought comfort. Those two people obviously thought, 'I'm going to send Sheryn flowers today.' I believe that's because they got a nudge from God.

When children go through pain or really tough times, it's the job of the parent to help them journey through. Offering advice if needed, encouragement, a listening ear or a shoulder to cry into. Sometimes a parent knows their child will be okay once they get through the situation, but that doesn't make the 'going through it' any easier.

Those flowers didn't change my circumstances, but they helped me feel I wasn't alone.

I also have to tell you about a life-changing conversation I had with God during this time. Remember I said at the start of this book that God guides me? This was one of those occasions. Did he speak to me audibly? No, but as I tell you about our conversation I hope you'll see it couldn't have been something I just made up in my head.

Brad and I had been trying to decide whether to put a second storey on our home. We lived in a cosy wee bungalow, but if it was going to be our family home, we needed to do some major alterations.

It was a Sunday afternoon in 2002 and I said to God, 'Here's the thing: I need to know if we should do the renovations on our house to ultimately raise a family here, because I don't want to do the renovations if we are not going to have kids.'

I also said, 'To be honest God, this is a really hard thing to deal with and I need some encouragement from you. I'm over all this not knowing and simply being labelled as infertile.' I was trying to deal with the embarrassment and shame I felt at not being able to have children. Let me say, no one made me feel bad, it was just how I felt.

So I was saying all this stuff to God. Some of it in my mind and some out loud, and then, really clearly, the phrase 'Isaiah chapter 54' popped into my head. This is a book in the Old Testament of the bible. I had no idea what Isaiah 54 said, so I looked it up and read chapter 54:1-4, (in a few different versions):

> 'Sing barren woman, who has never had a baby. Fill up the air with song you who've never experienced childbirth! You're ending up with far more children than all those childbearing women. God says so.' (MSG)

> 'Enlarge your house; build on additions, spread out your home! For you will soon be bursting at the seams!' (TLB)

> 'You're going to need lots of elbow room for your family.' (MSG)

> 'Don't be afraid, because you will not be ashamed. Don't be embarrassed, because you will not be disgraced. You will forget the shame you felt earlier.' (NCV)

Amazing!

Amazing verses in the bible — just for me. I was stunned. I guess I hadn't expected such a clear response.

This moment encouraged me that we would, in fact, have children. It gave me answers to those practical questions about doing renovations on our home. It also comforted me. I would forget my embarrassment, my shame. Now, you could be a sceptic and think, 'Nice coincidence', but I prefer to believe otherwise.

I hung onto those words from the bible. Again, did it suddenly take the pain away? No. Did I fall pregnant the next day? No. (Tayla wasn't born until 2006, and this was 2002.) But I did believe this was God speaking to me through his words in the bible, so what this did was give me hope.

As I said, Brad and I had attended meetings where we asked people to pray for us to have a baby. After our normal church service one Sunday, we drove to another small suburban church a friend had told us about. She said there was a couple visiting from overseas who were praying for people to be healed. 'Great,' I said. 'Let's go!'

Let me explain something. Whenever I asked people to pray for me, I was never expecting *them* to heal me. The healing, I believed, was only going to come from *God*. But the people who pray for healing sometimes have a huge amount of faith — a gift — and God uses them.

So Brad and I walk into a small, old-fashioned room, about the size of a school classroom.

There are a few chairs scattered around, but not in any particular order. There's no music, a few people milling around and a quiet buzz of chatter. In one corner is a line of about five people, all waiting to be prayed for. We join the queue.

When it's our turn, we find ourselves face to face with a husband and wife in their eighties. Not wanting to judge or sound rude, but they look old!

We sit on the school chairs in front of them. 'We can't have a baby,' I say simply. 'We'd like you to pray for us please.' By now, I'd done this so many times I don't get into long tearful explanations. I just make my very practical request.

It's like sitting with your very elderly nana and grandad, warm, weathered faces glowing back at you. They ooze love.

'What's the problem?' they ask. Again, I'm not up for giving them our full medical history, so I simply say, 'Brad had mumps when he was a teenager and I've got endometriosis.'

So, because I know God understands why we are here, I figure these people don't need a detailed explanation. The dear nana lady asks if she can place her paper-thin skinned hand on my stomach, and I say, 'Yes.' Thankfully, the grandad just places his hand on Brad's knee.

Then they pray. Very simply and calmly they ask God for healing. For my body and for Brad's. It takes about five minutes. When they have finished praying, they both sit there with their eyes closed for another minute or so.

I feel peaceful, but nothing else. Then the dear lady opens her eyes and through glistening tears says, 'Dear, God has given me a picture and I see two beautiful children coming from your womb.' (Remember that when you look at the pictures of my girls: 'two beautiful children'.) She senses God has given her that picture to share with me.

Yes, of course I cried. I can't remember if Brad did. (He says he didn't, but you know how men are!)

Why, you ask, didn't I just ask God for healing on my own? Why didn't I ask God for a picture of two beautiful children? Why did I ask so many others to pray for healing for me? Well, I did ask God to heal Brad and me, many times — many, many times! Sometimes I would feel peace. That yes, we would have a baby. Sometimes I would get a verse from the bible that would encourage me, or encouragement would come through others (as I mentioned in my flower delivery story).

But sometimes I think that because I was fully overwhelmed by my desires and pain, I couldn't actually 'hear' clearly from God. It was too hard to hear his voice and truths over what I and my thoughts were already consumed by.

I relate this to someone going to the doctor and hearing bad news. They say it's a good idea to take someone else with you for these sort of appointments, since once this news is heard a patient becomes so consumed by their new reality that they don't hear any more of what the doctor is saying. Whereas the friend is hearing, but listening with different ears. They are a little bit removed from the situation.

It really is a both/and situation. God could have given me my own picture of two beautiful children, but I may have doubted, thinking it was just my hopeful dream. So, to have someone else — who I believed was listening to God — say that she could see two beautiful children ... well, that gave me hope and encouragement. (I do want to say, though, that I don't have all the answers and I do still have a list of questions.)

Did I doubt over the next few years that maybe God didn't mean what I had read in the bible that day in 2002? Of course! I'm still human with emotions and hormones! It was in about 2003 or 2004 that we had prayer from this elderly couple. Again, Tayla wasn't born until 2006.

In hindsight, I remember asking God to help me through my doubting times and I realise now that just because I doubted his words and sometimes felt overwhelmed with sadness, that didn't stop him carrying out his plans for us. Thank God for that!

I'm always learning about patience. It's not something I'm too good at, but in saying that ... I am better than my husband!

I want to recount a more recent learning experience about hearing from God and having patience. Just because Brad and I had been through the IVF experience didn't mean we learnt perfect patience! We are always learning and growing.

So ... we were faced with selling a rental property.

We had owned the property for twelve years and just with timing and tenants it was time to sell. It took three months before we signed to accept an offer and despite weeks wondering, 'Will this ever sell?', we believed the timing would eventually be right. But the waiting wasn't easy.

I said to Brad that I felt when the money came through from the sale, we should give some of it away. He agreed. We both asked God in our own way where we should give the money to.

I have an amazing girlfriend who has served as a missionary overseas in places like Africa and Suriname. When she returned from spending three years in Suriname she had formed a close bond with two special women and their young children.

Without going into this too much, one morning Brad came back from a run and said, 'I think we should give [this] amount of money to one of those women in Suriname.' I agreed and felt this was totally right.

(Another side note: Remember I said I couldn't have married someone who didn't seek God's guidance for decisions in our life? This is just but one of many examples I could give of why I felt like that. Yes, I could have said the same thing to a husband who didn't believe in God, and he may have even come up with the same answer, but I would like to believe — and do believe — that God is guiding us as a couple. He sees a bigger picture than we do and so we trust him for guidance. As with our IVF journey and its timing, we seek God's guidance together.)

Back to the story ... Brad got in touch with my friend and we deposited the money into her account. She then emailed the lady in Suriname explaining about the money.

Well, the night before (in Suriname, on the other side of the world), this particular lady, now a solo mother through tragic circumstances, wakes during the night and is crying. She is crying out to God saying, 'Look at my house. I have no money and my house needs fixing. It doesn't need to be beautiful, but it does need to be better.'

And then, the next morning, she wakes to a message from my friend that an amount of money has been deposited into her account.

I was told she started crying again. Her wee boy comes in to see what's wrong with Mum and she is able to tell him the story of how she had cried out to God for help, and help has been given. That she can get his needed new shoes, some small gifts for Christmas — but more than that, her ceiling and roof, which desperately need fixing, can be repaired. She is so grateful because our gift is a tangible way for her to feel and know God's love for her.

A child calling to her father for help and practical help is given. Coincidence? The timing, the rental sale, the need, the donation? Think that if you like. But I don't.

Me? Totally different circumstances, but still calling out to God in my own sad desperation. My answers? Two bunches of flowers, and encouragement through friends' words, the bible and pictures from people I'd never met before. Perfect.

These are only a few stories — there are so many more. But for me this again and again confirms a God who does love us and is in control. Despite what we see and feel, he knows what is right and perfect for his children. And he does respond.

Every child is a thought in the mind of God, and our task is to recognise this thought and help it toward completion.

— Eberhard Arnold

The Baby

So I'm pregnant: what to do next? Well, for starters, we organise a specialist and a midwife. After going for a six-week scan and an appointment with the specialist we are told all is perfectly normal, so we leave the specialist behind and just stick with our midwife.

Next up: baby's room and all the trappings. Of course, we buy too much. More blankets than an Eskimo would ever need, more toys than any child could ever play with, and outfit after outfit. Oh, and the shoes. So cute! Babies don't even need to wear shoes, really. I mean, what walking do they do? But who cares? I needed to buy my baby shoes. We got everything we needed and far more.

Then: letting our friends know. We waited the obligatory twelve weeks before telling anyone outside our families. At the supposed safety of three months we host a dinner party. Our closest friends attend and are all sitting around in our lounge. Most of them are already first-time parents, or pregnant with round two.

Brad says, 'Ah, excuse me everyone, can you fill your glasses please, I'm going to propose a toast. Thanks so much for your friendship; we are so blessed to have amazing friends like you, especially with the journey we have been on. Oh and by the way ... [pregnant pause] ... we are finally having a baby.'

As brains compute this news, laughter, screams of delight, back slaps, hugs and tears.

I mentally step out of the room right now and see a snapshot of a moment I've never forgotten. Joy, relief, happiness, love, excitement and peace is expressed on the faces of our dear friends. *For us!*

They were on this journey with us. They had those moments of: 'When shall I tell Sheryn I'm pregnant?' 'How will I tell her it happened so quickly for us?' 'Shall I invite Sheryn to my baby shower?' All those moments, in one sense so hugely filled with joy for my friends, yet also so desperately filled with a thick and heavy sadness for me — now forgotten. History.

Every moment I can let people know I'm pregnant, I do. No floaty tummy-hiding clothes for me. No way! I proudly show off my steadily swelling belly.

I remember being at a wedding, wearing a pretty, figure-hugging dress. Appropriate, but still figure hugging. I was just over five months pregnant. A lady came up to me and said, 'You are obviously pregnant, how many months are you?' I loved that woman in that moment! I loved her for saying 'obviously pregnant'.

'Just over five months,' I glowed. 'It's my first.'

Not wanting to boast, but my pregnancy was a breeze. No morning sickness, no swollenness — apart from my belly. Cravings ... well chocolate lamingtons, but I have such a sweet tooth I think this was more an easy excuse than a fully authentic craving. Little mince pies, that was something new ... but yum!

The not sleeping part near the end of my pregnancy only meant there was a little life inside me that was squashing my internal organs into places they didn't usually sit. Space in my belly was becoming a competition, but I didn't mind.

When I was about eight to nine months pregnant, Brad and I went out for a walk one evening around our hilly suburb. We approached a set of stairs and were about to start up them when an elderly gentleman and his wife, also out walking, neared us. He smiled at me and said, 'You shouldn't be walking up those stairs in your condition.' Was I offended? No! He knew I had 'a condition'. I'd never had this condition before and I was loving every minute of it.

Names: again, so fun! What a responsibility, picking the name of a little person who would spend their life with that name. We thought about our own names and the meaning of them. How had our parents chosen them? Interesting conversations. Before we knew we were having a girl we had discussed names like Scarlett, Grace, Caitlin and Faith, but in the end were pretty sold on Tayla and/or Rylee. Boys we'd nailed down to Luke, Joel or Levi.

We named our daughter Tayla Faith. Tayla meaning 'gifted'. She is a stunning gift to us. 'Faith'? Obvious. It took a huge amount of faith to have our gift.

We knew at five months that we were having a girl, but didn't tell a soul.

As I've said already, IVF is a very public and invasive experience. The doctors, nurses and counsellors you must see are incredibly professional, but these are still other people involved in what is supposed to be a very private, intimate moment. Not for us. So the only way I felt I could have some control over this pregnancy was sharing things like the sex and name of our baby with Brad alone.

The due date approaches. Our midwife says, 'All is well, but your baby is in a posterior position.'

'Right ... and that means?'

She explains, 'Her head is down in the right position.'

'Yes, yes I feel that. I'm not waddling like a duck for no reason or just to prove my pregnancy!'

She says, 'Your baby's head should be face down, looking at the floor, but your baby is face up. It would be best if she turns into the normal position — posterior babies are much harder to push out.'

Due date tomorrow: We are going to have a baby tomorrow! We are finally going to be parents!

Due date arrives, baby doesn't.

As a child, you know when you are waiting for a special date to arrive and it never seems to come? Or as an adult, a long-awaited holiday approaches, but then for some reason, it doesn't happen? How do you feel? Let down, to say the least.

I had read the memo about how babies didn't always arrive on their due dates. Well, that wasn't going to be me. But it was.

Almost two weeks later: Seven years, forty weeks ... now a bonus two weeks.

At the check-up with the midwife, she says, 'If baby doesn't look like it's coming tomorrow, we are going to have to induce you.'

So, firstly, baby still has not turned despite my best efforts to make it happen. All the yoga-style positions I'd been told to sit, kneel and squat in for hours haven't paid off. Secondly, I have been trying everything in my power to get baby to come out. Fish and chips, they said. Didn't work. Have a hot curry, someone else told me. No good (although it was delicious). Cod liver oil, fast walking and all other physical moves prescribed. Just let me say, we tried it all.

Scan time: the twenty-fifth of May. Okay, baby is fine, still posterior, but it's time to help her out. 'I'm going to carry out a sweep', says my midwife. Another new term to learn about. Not my favourite. If you are a woman and have experienced one, you'll understand. Without too many details, what it means is the midwife wants to stretch you open and basically try to break your waters with her fingers to get things proceeding.

Sweep complete.

Friday, the twenty-sixth of May 2006. I wake about 5:30 am and realise my waters have just broken. Yay! This is a good sign.

I'd given up on my yoga moves as I'd been told baby could turn during labour, so ... hoping for that option.

I go for a walk — sorry, waddle — around the streets to keep my body busy and mind off the fact that sometime today I'm going to meet my baby. Can I just say that again? *My baby.*

Bags have been packed and ready to go for weeks. These are loaded into the car. About lunchtime I feel what I know to be a contraction. Let the games begin. It's more annoying than painful.

By 5 pm that evening, the contractions are enough to stop me in my tracks — and this is happening about every ten to fifteen minutes. Phone call to the midwife is made and she says, 'This is it. On your way to the hospital, Sheryn.'

You don't have to say that twice!

At the hospital we settle into a lovely suite filled with every contraption, device (and a pool!) that I may or may not want to try during birth. (Who knew?!)

Time passes: 6 pm, 7 pm. I've been on the Swiss ball, walking around, lying in different positions on the bed, not tempted into the pool, but I've tried everything else on offer. But still no sign of baby. Oh, don't worry, I'm still having contractions and I'm about 8 cm dilated, but baby does not want to come out.

I'm pushing as hard as I think I can. It's 9 pm, 10 pm ... baby is still posterior (although we didn't know that at the time). Midwife, I can tell, is starting to wonder what is happening — or not happening, more to the point.

I'd like to think I'm a strong person physically. I know I have a high pain threshold. I've had no drugs or gas, and every time the midwife says, 'push!', I do what I'm told. I'd get so far, excitement would build, baby is crowning, then ... contraction over, baby disappears. So frustrating! I am getting tired and the midwife says baby's heartbeat is quite fast now.

Late evening: 10:30 pm and the word 'forceps' is mentioned. Not happy. I mean, just picture forceps (not tweezers!) — an instrument that belong in a bloke's tool shed, not in my body!

As I said, up until this point, I've had no intervention ... and I'm not about to start now.

My husband whispers in my ear, 'You've got an hour-and-a-half left if you want our baby born on the 26th of May (Brad's father's birthday). Brad also knows I can't resist a challenge.

At 10:55 pm my midwife says to us, 'I'm going out of the room to get the specialist and it's time for forceps.' Those two incentives are all I need.

Next contraction I push with absolutely every ounce of my strength, determination and energy I have. And then a number of things happen that I didn't expect or plan for:

1. Yes, the hoped-for result, one baby's head, looking up — posterior like, of course — comes out.
2. I push so hard I fall unconscious, so I don't even know I've had a baby.
3. Because our midwife is out of the room, looking for said forceps, Brad realises it's just him, an unconscious wife and a baby's head on the bed.

At this stage he thinks some more help would be appropriate, so he presses a large red emergency button located on the side of the wall.

4. Midwives times three appear, plus a doctor and a specialist — all come running into the room.

5. I don't realise, but with the next contraction Tayla comes out. It's an 'oh!' moment for my midwife when she realises that because baby has been in the posterior position, she basically got stuck.

6. Lastly, as a bonus and because I pushed so hard with my last contraction, I also manage to push out a decent amount of my cervix. (I know; I never do anything on a small scale.)

When I regain consciousness, Tayla is lying on the bed being attended to by a midwife. There are two other midwives in the room as well as a specialist.

Brad says our baby's fine. Her face is a little munted after being stuck for so long face up in a place she shouldn't have got stuck. But she's okay.

Brad does the honours of cutting the cord. I'm just lying there, stunned. So not how it plays out beautifully in the movies. But the end result is a beautiful baby, albeit a bit beat up and bloody looking, one with a mass of dark black hair.

Despite her dramatic entrance, Tayla Faith Adamson, weighing seven pound two ounces, born at 11 pm, the 26th of May 2006, in my eyes is perfect. She's mine.

I thought my proudest moments were graduating as a police officer and getting married. This tops it off hands down. Brad sends out multiple texts to our dear friends and families, who, like us, have been waiting impatiently for baby's arrival.

Mum and my brother arrive to meet their first grandchild

and niece. Dad is out of town so has to wait a few more days to meet his granddaughter.

Despite her upside-down entry, Tayla is perfectly fine and ready for her first feed. The moment is surreal. I'm looking at Tayla and she's looking at me. It feels amazing. Yes, it has been traumatic and not at all what I expected, but this is the birth of my baby, so it's perfect.

Tayla, our gift, is passed to father, nana and brother as the specialist says he needs to make some running repairs now the placenta is out. 'Your cervix came out,' he says, 'and you have ripped yourself. A lot. I'm going to have to do quite a few stitches, but I will give you a local anaesthetic.'

Great, that sounds like fun after just giving birth. (I hope you're sharing my pain right now.)

The specialist, a lovely Thai man, sets up his spotlight and carries out the injections. Not good. My mantra at this point is: 'I'll pick up my dignity, along with my baby when I leave this hospital.' Now though, this hurts. It really does.

The specialist says, 'This will hurt.'

Yes, I can confirm that.

'I'm starting to sew you up now.'

'Okay that's good, concentrate please,' I say. My attempt at sarcasm is missed, perhaps lost in translation. He looks up at me a little strangely, and then his needle hits a part of me that has not quite been numbed.

I gasp.

'Um, don't look at me,' I say, 'just focus on what you're doing please, I'm fine.'

'Are you?' he says kindly.

'Yeah, never been better, just finish what you're up to please. I've got a baby I want to hold.'

After the spotlight is off and the specialist has gone, I finally feel more with it and I hold Tayla and look at her. Really look at her. Surprisingly, there are no tears, just peace, relief and proud joy. She's beautiful, perfect. (Like all babies, of course.) What a gift. What an honour. What a responsibility. She looks at me and smiles her first smile. (No she doesn't, that only happens in movies and novels. But she does look at me.)

My work is done, baby out safely. The room is quiet now and a peace and contentment I haven't felt in years settles over me.

This moment is blissful. All the pain, pressure and stress have gone. Family are in the room talking quietly, oohing and ahhing over the baby I've just produced.

Proud? One hundred per cent yes!

I won't lie; some of the next six weeks are a blur. Hard, tiring work.

Some of those times in the middle of the night when the bed is warm and the air is cold, when I'm tired and the rest of the house and neighbourhood sleep blissfully on, and I'm walking down the hallway to my crying baby to feed her. Sometimes this is really hard work — as much as I want this with all my heart. Other times, in the still of the night when it's just Tayla and me, watching her as she feeds. Bliss — tear-welling-up moments.

No one can prepare you for having a baby and all the change and emotions that come with that package. You just have to take every day as it comes and learn to enjoy the ride.

For a few weeks mastitis sets in. *Ouch and really ouch!* Tears well up for different reasons while breastfeeding.

Some would say Tayla was a good baby, sleeping six hours at six weeks, seven hours at seven weeks, and at the end of nine weeks we were getting about twelve hours of straight sleep!

But what's a good baby compared to a bad baby? Crying happens for a reason, doesn't it? That's Baby's only means of communication. Everyone is unique, as they should be. And so it is with babies and parenting styles, ideas and decisions.

Yes, I read books on pregnancy and childbirth. What to do, how to get baby to sleep, what I should eat while breast feeding, when to start solids, and all the other suggested do's and don'ts. Of course, I read it all. But ultimately, like most things in life, Brad and I worked out what was best for us by realising that parenting books are guides written by other people imparting the wisdom that worked for them. Some information was helpful, some not.

Does my daughter remember those nights when I was impatient with her? No. Those very early mornings when I had to put a pillow over my exhausted head and let her cry just a little longer to see if she would go back to sleep? No. I've actually asked her. She just knows she is a loved and very much longed-for daughter.

So in hindsight and with the wisdom of getting through the baby stage (twice), my encouragement would be: just do your best in love for your baby/children. Ask for help when you need it. Don't beat yourself up if you feel like the worst parent on the planet. Exhausted, unshowered, piles of washing everywhere, still in your PJs when bedtime rolls around again. Who cares? Your baby certainly doesn't!

Chalk it up to a parenthood experience that one day you will look back on and laugh about with your friends and children. I chose to just get on and enjoy and experience every aspect of parenthood, even when it wasn't pretty! The season will pass all too quickly. It doesn't always feel like it when you are in the middle ... but the season will change.

Faith is taking the first step even when you don't see the whole staircase.

— Martin Luther King Jr.

Get Knitting God

When Tayla turned one we decided it was time to get started on our next embryo. I was thirty-six, conscious of my age and very conscious of the fact that we still had three embryos left.

With embryo replacement the procedure is simple. Have numerous blood tests so the nurses can monitor where you are in your cycle. And then, at the most appropriate time, go into the surgery room and have an embryo replaced. No drugs, no self-inflicted injections, very simple and very painless (if you don't mind blood tests).

The first hurdle is: will the embryo unfreeze and be in an okay condition to replace? Our first 'ice baby', as I used to refer to them, was.

I went into the surgery room, along with Brad this time! Also joining us were two nurses, one embryologist, the specialist, and a very full bladder. This is probably the most uncomfortable part, especially when you have to relax to let a catheter-like tube be inserted to transport the embryo.

So I'm lying back with my feet in stirrups, the speculum in place and (ladies, you'll understand how uncomfortable this is) the TV monitor is on so everyone can see my insides. I'm getting used to my life being wide open! The nurses are ready, doctor is ready, my bladder is bursting, and we are just waiting for my embryo to arrive. It's a cosy wee room. (Whistle with me as you picture this pleasant scene! Again, this is our way of making babies.)

After a couple of uncomfortable minutes filled with nervous meaningless talk, finally the embryologist arrives, with a very long thin tube containing one of our defrosted ice babies. The doctor inserts this into my womb. I don't feel anything physically. We watch on the TV monitor as we see the tube appear, the embryo is 'ejected' into place ... and that's it. Over. I'm hopefully pregnant again. This time the bonus is Brad is present.

At this stage, 'normal' women trying to conceive would never even know that fertilisation has taken place. Yes, an egg may have been fertilised by a sperm, but you don't know if a pregnancy has resulted until about two weeks later when either your period does or doesn't arrive.

The difference for us is ... we do know. We've just watched a fertilised egg with all its stunning potential be inserted into its new warm home. We know there is a good chance, but we now just have to wait and see if it will 'stick' and grow.

It doesn't.

My period arrives the day my blood test is due. I'm devastated. I guess I thought, like Tayla's embryo, this one would work. It was a perfect embryo, so why wouldn't it?

I am surprised at how forcefully all my awful, painful infertility emotions come rushing back. I quickly became low in myself again, wanting to withdraw from friends and the world.

Girls in my antenatal group are falling pregnant for the second time and here I am again feeling like the odd one out. I know I should be extremely grateful for having one beautiful amazing baby. I am (truly!), but I've had a taste of motherhood and I want more.

All the while, that dear nana's voice is quietly whispering in my struggling mind, 'God has given me a picture and I see two beautiful children ...'

The month passes and I have the next round of blood tests. We return to the clinic at the appointed time, with full bladder on board, and watch as our next perfect embryo is replaced.

I don't need to wait for the blood test results this time. My period comes early. This time there are no tears. I've started to put up my protective emotional walls again. I haven't got my hopes up too high. Yet I still feel like I am grieving for two of my ice babies that I've lost and never got to meet.

The next month is the hardest emotionally. Going back to the fertility clinic for the last time my head is working overtime with all manner of questions. The main one being: 'If this doesn't work, can I start from scratch again with the IVF process? Can I go through this all over again?'

Brad is surprisingly at peace about this last time.

We get the call to say my body is ready and so is our last embryo, or 'blastocyst', as this one is called. Off to the clinic we go. Me, full bladder, Brad and Tayla. (Yes, Tayla was present when her potential sibling entered my womb.)

(An important side note here: This is the fertilised egg they weren't sure would develop properly. The odd one out amongst our four embryos. So this embryo, at day three when the others were frozen, was allowed to keep growing in a small, round petri dish, for a few days longer. They needed to see if it would develop and if the cells would keep dividing or not. It did keep growing and so was labelled a 'blastocyst'. The cells were dividing as they should. The embryologist said this last one had thawed and was looking good, so it was implantation time.)

Again, all goes well with the procedure, but then the harrowing wait begins again.

This time truly is the hardest of all emotionally. As my blood test approaches I am scared to go to the toilet in case I see blood. I'm not sleeping well and I'm often on the verge of tears.

On the Friday before the test, my dear friend Angela phones and I just lose it on the phone and blurt out what has happened over the past few months. She is so awesome and just listens. She can't do anything but listen and offer to be praying for me. And a sense of peace, despite the circumstances, does come.

Shouldn't I, a Christian, simply be able to rest in whatever God's will is and not get so worked up? Maybe, but reality is, I am a woman, with raging hormones and emotions, waiting for a desperately longed-for baby. (I've checked out my bible and there's quite a lot of lamenting in there, too. Often by some of the 'big guns'.)

So, no, I don't beat myself up. I feel what I feel, acknowledging God made us with emotions ... but I also tell God he'd better be 'knitting' flat out!

Let me explain what I mean by this. I was often reading Psalm 139:13,15 (NIV): 'For you [God] created my inmost being, you knit me together in my mother's womb. My frame was not hidden from you when I was made in the secret place.'

I am praying, 'God, figuratively, please knit me another baby!'

The day arrives. I have my blood test in the morning and then head home to wait for the all-important phone call, with results coming in around lunchtime.

I am keeping myself as distracted as possible and all is going well ... until about 11:30 am. I go to the toilet and find blood on the toilet paper. Saying my heart sinks is an understatement. Poor Brad gets a visual of the toilet paper and then has to deal with a weeping wife. He wisely says that just because there is some blood doesn't mean things aren't still good. But if this is bad news, we should keep looking at Tayla. *We were told we'd have no kids, and just look at our beautiful wee gift we have been blessed with!*

I know he is right, but it doesn't stop me from seasoning poor Tayla's scrambled eggs that I'm feeding her for lunch with my tears.

The phone rings right on 12 noon. I don't hesitate; I snatch it up just wanting to know.

Nurse: 'Is that Sheryn Adamson?'

'Yes.'

'Is it appropriate to talk now?'

'Yes!'

'Are you sitting down and ready for your results?'

'Yes!'

'Congratulations, you're pregnant.'

Well, that was it! The floodgates open yet again and I can't speak. Tayla, who is watching me and wondering what on earth is going on, starts to cry too, and poor Brad obviously thinks it is all over and I've just been given the bad news.

Without saying another word I manage to pass the now wet phone to Brad. He's expecting the worst. But soon he's saying, 'You're joking?!' as he hears he is going to be a father for the second time. Waves of relief pour out with my tears.

Reading over this last chapter I realise that I seem like a woman who is always weeping. Well, a lot of the time I was! The emotional roller coaster of IVF is massive. Experienced by thousands of hopeful couples all around the world month after month, this is a hard and draining journey, this way of 'making babies'.

I'd been a police officer for twelve years, having seen and dealt with stuff that I should have wept buckets over, but didn't. Yes, there were moments — and I've recounted a couple of these. But most of the time police just put up protective walls; otherwise we wouldn't be able to do our job.

What broke me about being labelled 'infertile' was my total lack of control about the situation. It's supposed to be normal/natural to make babies, but not for us (and not for thousands of others). We had no control over this one.

The IVF procedure made us totally dependent on others for their guidance, skills and direction — which was all brilliant, yet also entirely out of our hands.

I like to be in control. (I think I've mentioned that a few times.) So maybe this was a lesson I needed to learn, that I wasn't always going to be in control. This was a building exercise in faith and trust when the outcome was unknown and not controllable by me.

I learnt so much through those seven years, but I still often wonder: *why seven?* It felt like forever. For me, the greatest thing that came from this experience/journey (apart from my babies, obviously!) is my empathy.

> *Empathy: the power of entering into another's personality and imaginatively experiencing their experiences, power of entering into the feeling or spirit of something and so appreciating it fully.*

I have empathy and understanding in spades for women with endometriosis — their physical and emotional pain. Couples being told they are infertile, couples facing the dilemma of whether or not to do IVF, couples going through IVF, the emotional toll this takes. The list goes on.

I get it. It's hard. It feels unfair. For some it doesn't work! Too heartbreaking. *Why? More questions than answers, sorry.*

But — and I can honestly say this — I wouldn't change that empathy for anything. Easy to say in hindsight, of course. But if someone goes through something and doesn't learn from it, doesn't grow, isn't able to help others, and let the journey shape them to be a better person ... well, that would be a waste, wouldn't it?

And I don't like waste.

God was knitting. It just took time though.

Don't cry because it's over, smile because it happened.

— Dr Seuss

Round Two And Beyond

Rylee, like her personality, had different plans about her arrival. Due date: Thursday the 17th of April 2008.

I know she is in the launch position and it's her due date. But all I can remember is waiting two, long extra weeks for her sister to arrive. Thankfully, this is not to be with Rylee. At 5 pm on Monday the 21st of April 2008, Brad and I and nearly two-year-old Tayla are sitting having dinner together at the table. 'Oh,' I say, 'that felt like a small contraction.'

A few more contractions throughout dinner, nothing to stop me eating, but just enough to let me know something is happening. I'd experienced the aforementioned 'sweep' with my midwife earlier that day and she had predicted: 'I'll be very surprised if your baby doesn't arrive tonight.'

By 8 pm, Tayla is in bed and well asleep. Brad and I are halfway through watching a DVD. 'I think I'll just ring the midwife and give her a heads up about what I'm feeling.' She's not surprised when I call.

'I'm having a few contractions and I'll probably be calling you a little bit later.'

'Don't leave it too late,' she warns.

Mum, who has been on standby to come and stay with

Tayla, gets her phone call that it is probably time for her to come over to our place. Our car is again packed and ready to go. We continue to watch the end of the DVD and by now I'm having to stand to walk through the stronger contractions I'm feeling. It's uncomfortable, but not too bad.

The DVD finishes at 8:30 pm. Mum arrives and I have a pretty strong contraction. Brad rings the midwife and we decide it's time for round two. Mum prays with us and off we go. I'm in the back seat with more strong contractions.

We arrive at the entrance to the hospital at 8:50 pm — again, having to stop walking because of the force of the contractions. Midwife is there waiting.

I carefully climb onto the bed and a heart monitor is placed around my huge, swollen belly. My midwife wants to take a sample of my blood to check something, but I say, 'You'll just need to wait a moment,' as another contraction sweeps over me.

It's 9 pm. Brad takes a photo of me on the bed and then starts to sort out my suitcase. Before my midwife can get the needle in my arm I say, 'I need to turn over.' Onto my stomach, on all fours, I say, 'I think my waters have just broken, Brad, you need to get my pants off.' I'm still fully dressed. I've only had time to get my shoes off and clamber onto the bed.

Once Brad and the midwife have managed to manoeuvre off my track pants, she announces the blood test won't be happening at this time 'as your baby's head is out'.

'We are having a speedy birth in here — need some help please!' yells my midwife.

'Oh'.

Next push at 9:10 pm, Rylee McKenzie Adamson is born in a rush.

No control over this one and only one semi-push required.

I think a sneeze would have worked. Rylee has made a quick decision that it is time to come out. So she does.

However, because of her speedy entrance, she is stunned, very purple and not breathing.

A doctor has come into the room and wraps Rylee up. Brad is told to quickly cut the cord, which he does. Then Brad, doctor holding purple, bundled-up Rylee, and a nurse all literally run out of the room.

I'm left alone, at least conscious this time, with my midwife beside me. Again, not how I pictured the delivery going. No baby-on-tummy moment. I'm left to push out my placenta and then my midwife says, 'Well, I may as well just do a few stitches.'

Why not? Nothing else to do.

Brad, instinctively and protectively, is trailing behind the doctor who is holding our brand-new daughter in his arms. Brad enters a room filled with all sorts of machines to find purple, lifeless Rylee lying on a bed. Her wee body — all seven pounds, three ounces of it — is surrounded by medical staff, all working incredibly efficiently and purposefully to get this girl to take her first breath.

There is urgency, but no panic.

Meanwhile, back in my room, my midwife is gently stitching me up, all the while talking about how good the doctors are and that baby will be fine. I'm so grateful for this distracting, encouraging commentary from my brilliant midwife.

It takes a good few minutes before Rylee finally starts to breathe on her own. She is returned to me, carried in the arms of her very relieved and proud dad. She is still purple and has bloodshot eyes because of the force with which she arrived. But again I have another perfect baby. Mine.

Rylee today is my decisive child. Makes up her mind

quickly about what she wants and then acts on it. Whether it be what to buy, wear or do — decision made, action done.

Rylee had decided it was her time to arrive and nothing was going to get in her way of coming out that birth canal. *No sir, it's my time!*

Tayla, as with her birth, needs to weigh up all the options presented to her. This can make shopping for anything a very lengthy process. All shops must be visited first, followed by discussions about all the items she has seen, before something is bought. This was reflected in her *shall I come out? shall I not come out? I like to see what's going on first* birth experience!

Rylee and I spend four nights in hospital to make sure her breathing is fine, and they also keep an eye on my blood levels. This is a special time for Rylee and me to bond (not that she thanked me for it or anything!) after her rapid entry into the world.

Everyone says time with your little ones goes so fast, so make the most of it as you'll never have those special moments again. And it does. Sometimes.

I look at my tweenaged girls now and most days I say to them, 'Please stop growing!' (They roll their eyes back at me, of course.)

I ask them, 'Please hold my hand when we walk down the street, not because you have to, but because you want to.' *I want you to!* Most of the time, at the moment, I get 'Muuuum' ... but then a small, soft hand holds mine as if to humour me. I don't care, I love it!

However, there were times — usually in the middle of the night, exhaustedly getting up for feeding time — when I would think, 'I don't know if I can do this again and again and again, knowing there will be a busy toddler waiting for me in just a few hours.'

Tiring, hard, emotionally and physically exhausting sometimes. All-consuming and hard to see the way forward.

I'm being honest, because there were times when I would think, 'I just can't wait till she sleeps through the night, till she stops breast-feeding (I actually loved this and did it for both girls till they were one — but it was draining being their food supply), till we can go out and not have to pack a suitcase just to get to the supermarket and back. These were moments along the journey.

It's about finding the balance between enjoying this time and realising I am not and never will be Supermum.

But my girls don't want Supermum — they just want *their mum* to be present, available and love them with every ounce of her being. Which I try to ... and therefore, I guess, that does make me Supermum in their eyes.

Those moments, with all their stresses, funny stories, not having that spare nappy when baby explodes out the back all over their white jumpsuit ... priceless, beautiful moments I will forever treasure in my heart. (Funny now, not so much at the time!)

Normal, I would suggest, for a human being — especially a new mum — to feel tired and to long for *just one moment* to not feel depended on. (I see you nodding your head with me ... I thank you for your support.)

Children are totally precious gifts that are sometimes also lots of hard work.

Then along comes crèche at two-and-a-half years. One morning a week for three hours. Weird, leaving my baby in the care of another, albeit wonderful, caring and capable women.

Brad and I decided I would be a full-time mum. Yes, sacrifices would need to be made, especially financially. And life would look different for a while. But this was for a season — a season we had longed for and one we wouldn't get again.

Crèche followed by kindergarten. Each stage gifting my children with new independence. I feel so grateful my daughters were happy to head off to kindy without tears. My heart would break for mums with little ones who didn't want Mum to go — Mum needing to get away, child clinging on for dear life.

These times conjured up memories of my dealings with Mary. Nowhere near the same, of course, knowing these children would be happy within minutes of Mum leaving and Mum would be back in four hours. *Not so for Mary.*

First day of school. So much excitement! So many nerves ... for me, of course!

The blessing of living just three minutes' walk from the girls' primary school means most days it's just out the door and walking to school the 'old-fashioned way'.

We'd been on school visits, meeting the teacher, getting a feel for the classroom and how the days would play out. Tayla saying she was excited and ready for school. A major understatement. There was no indecision about this moment. She was off!

The teacher greets us, shows Tayla where her bag and coat go. She is off to play with a few children she's already met on past visits. Then the bell rings.

Time for Tayla to say goodbye. I feel the anxiety building within me. This is a significant moment. My child will spend more daytime hours with lots of other little people. She will be guided by other adults now. Don't get me wrong, all the girls' teachers have been fantastic. It's just ... well ... I'm their mum!

As I move in to say, 'I love you, have a great first day at school,' for the umpteenth time, my dear five-years-and-two-days-old daughter sees my face and I can almost hear her sigh. She sees me fighting back the tears and is hoping not to be embarrassed by her mother.

Tayla places her soft hands on either side of my cheeks, looks directly into my eyes with her stunning hazel ones, and says in her most grownup of voices, 'Mummy, I think it's time for you to go home now.'

Gulp.

'Okay Tayla. Love you.'

And just like that ... I am dismissed. My schoolgirl is in no need of a weeping mother hanging around to help. She is ready and capable of doing all that is required of a five-year-old.

I walk out of the class, behind Brad, who is carrying Rylee. I don't look up, not wanting to catch anybody's eye. Straight out the school gates ... and then the floodgates open — really open — and I literally cry all the way home. All three minutes' walk.

First child going to school, done. Her time at home as a toddler, done.

Second-time around, it was a different sad emotion. Now there were to be no more babies at home.

Rylee, just like her big sister, totally ready to start school. No asking me to stay after the bell; just completely willing and ready to start her new adventure.

Kisses and hugs, and for me tears welling up again. Rylee saying, 'See you Mum. Love you.' Then watching me, pushing me out the door with the movement of her encouraging blue eyes and sweeping movements of her hands to help me exit.

I've been mummy helper in both the girls' classes throughout their primary years. Mummy helper on trips to the zoo, beaches, parks and museums. So fun watching your children develop their own unique personalities. All these memories and moments I treasure and seal away.

It's hard to let your children go, so to speak, even though they are only three minutes down the road.

Brad and I are raising our girls to be confident in

themselves, in who they are, what they look like, in their personalities, and in what they believe. To celebrate their strengths and work on things they don't find so easy. I'm proud that, thus far, the way they handle themselves and situations shows they're maturing into confident, well-rounded girls.

On the other hand, my protective nature — the ex-police officer, the mother, the nurturer, the lioness — she wants her babies to need her. She wants to 'hover' over them so nothing and no one can hurt them. She almost wants her babies to say, 'Don't go, mummy!' But they don't. I need to be happy about this, and I am ... yet it's hard sometimes. Change and letting go often are.

So, what does one do when the babies have departed and headed off to school? I found out that life, somehow, seems to be just as busy, but different.

I talked about a seed being planted way back when I was first looking to join the police. Well, it had obviously been well watered and now was the time for it to blossom.

But first, my body. My insides still needed some major attention.

Be thankful for what you have; you'll end up having more. If you concentrate on what you don't have, you will never, ever have enough.

— Oprah Winfrey

21

Inside Issues

Let's deal with the insides first and then work our way out.

So, how does one end the long, painful and sometimes debilitating journey with infertility and endometriosis? Well, a full hysterectomy would go a long way to doing that.

Now blessed with two babies, no more embryos to give a chance to, and two more laparoscopic surgeries later, my body was saying enough is enough. Pain was creeping into my life again and I knew it was time for another, possibly last visit to my gynaecologist, whom I'd now known for nearly fifteen years.

She had kindly, yet quite forcefully said (and I love her for this), 'Next time I operate on you, my dear, I'm taking the lot out. It's done its job.'

End of 2015, one month till Christmas and I know my insides are not right. You get to know what 'tweaks' and pains are not normal. I make an appointment on a Thursday to see my specialist. Fourteen days later I find myself, with husband and suitcase in tow, at 6:00 am, standing before the doors of Wakefield Hospital in Wellington ready for a full hysterectomy, removal of my appendix and gallbladder, and to fix a hernia!

Am I nervous? No. Truly no. I've never felt more at peace. Sad, yes. My surgeon is going to remove the part of me where my two beautiful daughters lived and grew for nine months each. Six body parts are being taken out of me and that seems a bit weird, but no nerves.

We are greeted by a lovely nurse called Maggie. Maggie is the perfect balance between friendly and professional. Relaxed, yet working and moving with the efficiency of a nurse who has done this many, many times over.

Arriving at 6:00 am, by 7:30 am prepared like a lamb to the ... (joking!), I'm wheeled outside the theatre doors ready to go to sleep. The only time I start to well up is when Brad kisses me goodbye. (He still has that effect on me.)

My lovely anaesthetist says, 'I'm just going to give you something to help you relax and enjoy yourself.' All the while, he and the theatre nurses are keeping up their distracting relaxed chatter. And it's in that moment I go to sleep. No being rolled into theatre or counting to ten. I think my body is so at peace and ready for this moment that I just sleep.

At 8:30 pm, I open my eyes in recovery. It's been twelve hours of full-on surgery. But it's done. Six body parts removed and it's like I'm just waking from a lovely deep sleep.

Despite the fact that I have a drip line attached to one arm, catheter in place, pumps on both my legs to keep the blood flowing, oxygen being pumped in through tubes up my nose, and my face and body hugely swollen from the fluid being pumped into me, I'm in no pain and I look semi-normal. It's done.

'You don't look like our mum,' comments my seven-year-old the next day on their first visit to see me. *Oh. So maybe I don't look semi-normal after all.*

Here's something awkward that might give you a chuckle at my expense. You remember how I said I truly felt relaxed pre-operation? Well it's true, apart from one brief moment.

Back to my nice pre-op nurse Maggie. She has gone through all the bits and pieces she needs to do before the lucky last job: an enema. *Great. Never had one before, hoped not to ever have one.* But Maggie has to make sure the way is 'clear', so to speak, before operating.

Picture this (not too graphically, but let your mind wander a bit to my situation): I'm now clothed in my lovely dark blue, back-opening, hospital gown. Lying on my left side, butt bare, being told to relax. Easier said than done! Yes, there is some anxiety at this moment.

Then the cold tube, like a thin thermometer, is placed where it needs to go. And then ... a phone rings. Not just any phone; the cordless phone Nurse Maggie has in her uniform pocket. The phone must be answered ASAP. Maggie is in charge and this call may be urgent. Here I am, butt-naked, tube inserted and Maggie says, 'I'm very sorry, Sheryn. The timing's awful, but I have to take this call.'

'Go right ahead,' I say, 'I'm not going anywhere!'

One of her hands is holding the tube in place, the other is pressing buttons on the phone, and in her most professional voice she sing-songs, 'Good morning and welcome to Wakefield Hospital.' *Not so much a good morning for me right now,* I'm thinking. I know Brad is having a great chuckle to himself in the corner as this comical scene plays out.

Uterus, cervix, tubes, one ovary, infected and inflamed appendix, and gallbladder removed. A twisted bowel fixed. More endometriosis removed. Cysts removed and a hernia fixed. My surgery was long, and the hazy recovery time of six weeks frustratingly longer. A special part of me was removed along with some bonus pieces, and my body had a lot of readjusting and healing to do.

But as my surgeon had said, my womb had done its job well, housed two children and now was only causing pain. *Time for you to go. Auf Wiedersehen,* as Heidi Klum would say! Let that season come to a complete and final end. It did ... or so I thought.

In fact, this was an operation that kept on giving.

After six weeks' rest, which I thought I had done very well, I was back to the surgeon for the all-clear. *Wrong. Oh, so totally wrong!*

Once I hit about three weeks into my six weeks' recovery I was starting to feel a little better. You'd expect this, of course. I had finally come off the three lots of drugs I had been taking morning and night. I had stopped injecting myself each night with a small, yet surprisingly stinging needle. The swelling was slowly going down and I could see my toes again while standing.

My husband and children were taking care of my every need. Yet, in my mind, I wasn't resting. I was frustrated with my body. Frustrated I couldn't do what I wanted to do. Longing and planning to get out of the house for just a little walk up the street. How could I speed up getting back to my 'normal' life?

One warm, windless morning, after a great nine hours' sleep overnight, my husband and two friends have gone for a run. It's such a nice day. *Just a tiny walk*, I think. I gingerly put on normal clothes instead of the PJs I've been wearing day and night since coming home.

Out the front door and I feel good. I literally shuffle about 50 metres up the street and back. It feels good to be 'doing' again.

I didn't do any more walks, not wanting to push my luck. I also remember having a few sneezing attacks — probably all those lovely flowers sent by so many kind people. But sneezing puts pressure on internal stitches. So I'm back in stirrups at my six-week check-up and things are not good. I have a major tear in my stitches and internal tissue. You have to remember this is about my fifth operation now, and my surgeon says, 'Your insides are like stitching up wet pieces of tissue paper.'

We are about to go on a family summer holiday and even though I know I wouldn't be running, I'm now told I can't swim. We are a beach family. We love to swim. I love to swim with my children.

Driving home from the appointment, husband and beautiful children do their best to console upset wife and mother.

'At least you are still allowed to go on the holiday.'

True.

'At least you can still sit on the beach and watch us swim, Mum.'

True.

'At least you can still eat ice-cream.'

So true.

Many things I can't do. But many things I can — I am so grateful for this reality check from my children. So I dry my tears and put on my grateful hat. Not quite the same as my running cap or swimming cap, but I'm determined to stay grateful.

Returning from a wonderfully special family holiday I'm booked in for more surgery. This operation happens one evening and only takes about an hour.

My surgeon says, 'Before I operate and stitch you back up, I need to check there is no infection. If there is, I can't operate; but if there is no infection, we operate.' *Fair enough.*

This surgery is different from my last. I walk into the operating theatre, wearing my fabulous blue gown and the anaesthetist helps me up onto the operating table. My surgeon is in the room along with three other nurses.

It's like we are all getting ready to shoot a scene for the TV hospital drama *ER*, apart from George Clooney not starring as Doctor Doug Ross. He is not here. (Unfortunate, some of you sigh. I digress, but humour helps me get through this.)

I'm lying on the operating table, covered in sheets. Legs up in stirrups, yet again. Did I mention that thing called 'my dignity'? Well, I did get it back after childbirth, but it's gone by the wayside again. In fact, it's hanging in some back cupboard throughout this whole experience. I'm not sure when I'll find it again. Least of my worries.

The surgeon has put the speculum in place. Now she is directing the nurse in control of the huge mobile light to shift it into a better place so she can see more clearly. This takes time and quite a bit of direction. Sometimes this direction is agitated, sometimes more calmly spoken.

The surgeon/director is focused and knows what she wants. The lighting nurse is doing her best. Sound nurse is near my head; hand on my shoulder and saying all the right comforting words. Props nurse is lining up on a table beside my surgeon all manner of silver, torturous-looking devices. The instruments of the trade: scalpels, scissors, clamps and needles.

Meanwhile, the anaesthetist, who has a seat beside my head on the other side of the sound nurse, has kept up a lovely babble of constant chatter. You know how when some people are nervous or feeling uncomfortable, they talk? This was him, in a nice way, though.

He is reassuring me. He's saying things like, 'Don't worry, I'm going to stay up by your head while all the other stuff is happening.' He adds, 'Please do tell me to be quiet if I'm talking too much, but this is a bit awkward you see. Usually my patients are asleep while all this is happening.'

'Awkward?' I reply. 'Well, how about we swap places and then let's see who feels more awkward?' He has a wee laugh.

Director: 'Tilt her backwards so I can see better.'

Props nurse tilts the operating bed backwards. Ooops! I

nearly slip backward, head first off the bed with this sudden dramatic downward angle.

Director: 'Too much, too much!'

I agree because now I can see up my anaesthetist's nose and I feel my legs starting to slowly slide out of the stirrups. The bed and I are quickly tilted back and calm is restored. The director continues with her work.

The anaesthetist had wisely placed his hand on my head during this dramatic shot, so I couldn't have actually gone flying off the wrong end of bed. *Grateful for the small things!*

'Are you okay?' he whispers. Very concerned look on his face.

Fine, a stunt double would have been better for that scene, but I handled it. No, I didn't really say that. I just smile (trying not to cry, I'm starting to feel a little anxious now) and reply, 'I'm fine.'

However, he does pipe up, with a little 'Ahem' to remind the director that the star of the show is very much fully awake and aware of what is going on.

Director: 'Yes. I know.' Very focused.

I'm uncomfortable, physically and emotionally. But I'm used to it by now, and because of the position I'm in I literally can't do anything about it, so I'm doing the best I can to be grateful. These people are here to help and make me better.

Director: 'There's no infection, I'm ready to start work, so put Sheryn to sleep.'

Sighs of relief from everyone in the theatre — including me on the bed. The anaesthetist is obviously delighted he no longer has to support a 'live' patient. He quickly says, 'I'll pop the needle in your arm and give you something to put you out. You will be asleep, although you may become slightly aware of voices during the procedure. But don't worry, you won't feel anything.'

'Ah, I'd rather not hear voices, so a good strong dose of

your special medicine would be appreciated. Can you keep that in mind please?'

He does, bless. I wake an hour later in the recovery room none the wiser as to how the director called the shots as the rest of the scene played out.

The tear/hole is far larger than my surgeon first thought. She tells me there is no way my body could have healed itself, so more stitching was absolutely necessary. She then makes it very, very clear that it has to work this time or we are looking at reconstructive surgery under general anaesthetic — an absolute last resort and not her desired plan of attack.

No, I agree, *I'm done with starring in medical dramas.*

So, added to my list of not walking (I learnt to shuffle like granny around my house) and no swimming, is no belly laughing, no coughing and no sneezing. I want to ask if breathing is allowed, but realise I'll probably laugh, which will get me a telling-off from my surgeon, so I keep that question to myself.

I am loaded up for the next six weeks with drugs for pain, drugs to stop infections, and drugs to stop me from sneezing. It's a shame there are no drugs to stop belly laughing. They would have been helpful as well.

After three days of being home, I am sitting outside enjoying the sun. I watch as my sixteen-year-old cat Benson jumps up onto the spa pool on our deck. In the summer we fill the spa with cold water and the kids use it as a pool. We don't usually put the lid on it during the day when they are at school.

But Benson, probably suffering from dementia (being one hundred and twelve in human years and all) has forgotten this and jumps up to lie in the sun on the spa lid, which isn't there. He gets a cold, wet shock. Being an invalid, I can't jump up and help fish the poor guy out, but he manages to haul his waterlogged body to the side of the spa pool and

clamber out. He then lines up close by my chair and leaps
— but misjudges!

You know how as you get older the mind is still willing
and able, but the body is not? That was Benson's reality.

His front paws and claws land and desperately try to
grip the armrest of my wooden chair, but his miscalculation
means he smacks his chin (if cats have chins) on the arm
of the chair. Benson's claws can't hold his weight, and like
a slow motion of nails down a blackboard, he slides then
slumps to the ground.

I've managed to shuffle over to his location by this time
and see he is shaking himself off more in embarrassment
than pain. He's letting me know he is not happy, but I'm
obviously making a strange noise, so he struts off to clean
himself up.

Those strange noises? My attempt to not belly laugh at a
scene so incredibly funny!

So, back on six weeks' bed rest, round two. (I know. There
are no words. Thank you for pitying me.) In all honesty, the
second time around I learnt a lesson that I plainly didn't
learn well enough the first time round.

I am no longer constantly thinking: 'Do I feel like I could
just do a little walk, have just a little bit of exercise, even
though the surgeon said no?' 'Do I feel like I could help by
hanging out that washing, even though the surgeon said
no?' 'Do I feel like I could just tidy that cupboard, just pick
up those toys?' (You get the picture.)

This time I was very, very good. I was learning to give
myself permission and time to let my poor battered body
rest. Time just to be. To be still, read, write, colour-in (all
the craze for adults at the time), to sit and talk to my girls.
Time to sit outside and watch the tui birds, the butterflies,
and whatever shapes the clouds were making that day. Time
to be still — and grateful.

So many lovely texts and emails from friends and family would include a line from the bible: 'Be still and know that I am God' (Psalm 46:10, NIV). And so I did.

I learnt to rest and rest well. To be at peace with my situation. Remembering my lessons of being grateful. I am so grateful my body will heal when many, many people have bodies diagnosed with all manner of diseases that won't heal.

I am so grateful for the beautiful people in my life who text encouraging messages. Who send flowers, bake meals and treats.

I am so grateful for those who send cards and notes just to say they love me, that they are praying for me and thinking good healing thoughts for me.

So grateful for those who had our children over for play dates to give Brad a rest.

Even grateful for the dear friend who dropped off a ukulele and music book so I could learn how to play it while resting. (I kid you not!)

So grateful for my Bradley John. I'm so blessed with a husband who is a fabulous cook and so graciously cares for me. Such an awesome hands-on dad to our girls. That marriage vow 'in sickness and in health' was tested hugely through this time — and we made it. Brad passed with flying colours. *So grateful!*

God whispers in my ear one morning as I am practising being still. I roll over in bed and realise my husband had gone for yet another early morning run, which used to be my favourite time for running. God whispers to me, 'A strong mind is better than a strong body.'

'Too true,' I say back to God.

'I know,' he says, 'that's why I said it.'

God does speak to me like that. No, not audibly, but I know his voice. It's friendly and funny (not that I was allowed to belly laugh or anything). God knew those thoughts that were starting to creep in and that could threaten my recovery ... *if only I could run ....*

God knows I like to keep fit and healthy — and there is nothing wrong with that. He knows I like a tidy house. He knows I like to feel I'm pulling my weight with the jobs that need to be done. But what I've needed to learn is the wisdom of balance. Letting my body heal and not keeping on pushing it to see if I can get a bit more out of it. This is wise.

I'm blessed. I will heal. I will walk and maybe run again, albeit a little slower and a little less. Some people won't. I need to remember this. I'm learning wisdom, patience, gratefulness, and being still-ness. I'm learning to not rush (I think Doctor Libby Weaver would say amen to this). Learning I don't have to be everywhere. I don't have to be everything to everyone.

Surprisingly, life goes on. Life hasn't stopped just because I have. It's actually become more peaceful, which is nice.

Life dishes out many opportunities to learn different lessons. This time around, I decided, I was going to learn.

No experience is wasted … everything in life is to grow you up.

— Oprah Winfrey

My Time To Shine

After having my girls and seeing them transition safely into their school years, I started toying with the idea of re-joining the police. I think I knew deep down, though, that as much as I absolutely loved the job, being a mum had changed me.

It took Brad and me so long to have children that I wanted (and want) to spend as much time with them as possible. Before school, after school, being mummy helper and being a taxi driver for all the things they were involved in. I wanted to do that.

Becoming a parent changed my priorities. As a police officer, hand on heart, I would have done anything, even given my life, to help protect people or to back-up a fellow officer in whatever situation we found ourselves. Hand on heart, I would do that now for my girls. The lioness in me would come to the fore.

But now? I could not say with all surety that I could fully give myself to the role of a front-line police officer. I would think about my girls' lives without their mum and I couldn't do that by choice. Lots of women can and do, and I take my hat off to them. But that wasn't an option for me anymore. With all that police officers must deal with these days and the thought of going back to shift work, that door was shut. Well, in one sense.

God, my Heavenly Father, knows the deepest desires of my heart. He knows what I'm passionate about. He knows how much I loved being a police officer. (He also knows when I look longingly at that expensive pair of shoes or just another new dress how strong that desire is!) God made me, and along my journey, he has shaped me. He gets me more than I understand myself. And so I feel he blessed me with a dream job. Well, three actually.

First dream job: finally being a mum. And mums will know that this is probably the busiest, hardest unpaid job anyone can ever do. We are still a wife, friend, daughter, maybe sister and auntie, but add to that mum, nurse, counsellor, taxi driver, house cleaner, gourmet chef, chief picker-upper, and fountain of all knowledge as to where everything is in the house — in which drawer and at all times. Love it!

And second dream job: I now do contract work at the Police College. Along with a group of mainly ex-police officers, I carry out role playing with recruits. One week, I might be the victim of a burglary and the nice policeman or woman has to come and take my burglary complaint. The next week, I'm a witness to an incident and give feedback on how well they take my statement.

A fun week is when I get to be an offender. I may have a knife in my shoe, some drugs in my pocket, or tools I'm about to use to commit a burglary.

I can get arrested, searched and handcuffed up to twelve times a week without so much as a rap sheet. So much fun! I also mark some of the paperwork that the recruits produce. (Less fun, but still ...)

Police College remains a positive yet stressful environment. I see these young-looking, keen recruits and it takes me back. I see my own face in theirs. I get to experience the feeling over and over of starting out on a dream job.

Yet, at the end of the day, I can go home to my children knowing I won't be dealing with pain and suffering. It's contract work, so come the school holidays, my number-one dream job of being a mum takes priority. But such an unexpected and amazing blessing.

My third job: A business I started myself. Remember the seed I said was sown when the recruiting sergeant looked me up and down and said 'You can't be a police officer'? Well, I can and I will — and I did, thank you very much! (Sorry, that may have been uncalled for.)

Anyway, for years while I was in the police, I would go shopping with some of the guys from my squad on our days off, looking for that 'tidy casual' outfit. They would say to me, 'Sheryn, I can wear the uniform or a suit, but I'm going on a date and I don't know what to wear.'

'Let me help you,' I'd say. And we'd go shopping together.

I realised I was able to see what worked on people and what didn't. What colours made people look good and what drained them. What a shirt could do if it was cut right. Or why some styles of trousers worked and some didn't. When shopping with a girlfriend or my mum, they would try on different styles of dresses and some looked amazing, but others didn't flatter their shape at all.

In 2010, after much online research and organising with my mum and husband to look after the girls, I spent two full weeks, 9 am to 5 pm, training to become an Image, Colour and Style Consultant. The intensive course was directed by Clare Maxfield, who runs the International Styling Company based in Australia. She, too, is a style consultant — and much more. She travels the world training people like me and giving talks to all manner of companies in regards to all things stylish.

Clare's training helped me understand the 'why' behind what I was seeing. Why some colours worked for people but others didn't. Why different body shapes and proportions needed different clothing styles. What 'style personalities' are, and why it's important to know yours.

Look, I get passionate when I start talking about this, so I'll leave it at that— but suffice to say that if, after reading this, you think you need help with your wardrobe and you live in Wellington, check out my website, www.sherynadamson.com.

What gives me so much pleasure in this work (and you may be surprised by this) is that it's not about the clothes; it's about when clients put on styles and colours that suit them, which I've chosen for them to try, and then they look in the mirror. To see their faces, this is what drives me!

To see confidence, self-worth and self-acceptance grow. Realising that despite what magazines might say about my shape, style and size, that despite that self-deprecating voice in my head that speaks far too loudly, actually ... I look and feel pretty good right now!

And that's why I do what I do.

For clients to realise that without spending mega dollars, without having to lose ten kilos, without having to get cosmetic work done, they look fabulous in their own skin. It's such a buzz! It is about being mindful of the client's lifestyle, who they are as a person, and how they want to present themselves. Putting all that together, it's honestly a humbling privilege to see men and women looking in the mirror and having a cry (women only at this stage) because they know they look great.

All of us are too hard on ourselves. Women especially. We look in the mirror and see faults. It doesn't help that society is so driven by 'looks'. I'm saying 'we' here because I'm very much including myself in this observation. So, if by doing what I do, I can make a difference to just one person, that's gold! That's a dream job right there.

I often do speaking engagements to different groups and audiences. Yes, I get nervous, but at the same time I love it. Because I'm passionate about the topic, the words flow easily. I'm in preaching mode. (Just like Mum and Dad!) I usually start off by saying, 'First impressions count.' How we present ourselves, head-to-toe, clothing, shoes, hair, makeup, accessories ... all gives off a message about us. Rightly or wrongly.

It's said that people make a judgement call about others within three to five seconds of meeting. That's before we even open our mouths! So how you present yourself tells your story even before you get to speak. Yes, it's unfair. But it's also how human nature is.

I do it and I've done it. During my time as a police officer it was a job requirement. And I still do it now. It's a habit, deeply ingrained. Human nature, as I said. And now I also make judgement calls from an image consultant's point of view. But we all make these judgement calls. It's not wrong; it's actually a good survival tool. But my big thing is what we do with those calls. Do we throw stones or not?

My then Miss two-and-a-half-year-old Rylee. Sitting at the breakfast bar busy watching her dad cook dinner. 'What are you cooking for dinner, Daddy?'

Brad picks Rylee up and takes her over to the oven top. He says, 'What do you think we are having?'

Rylee looks in the frying pan and her face recoils in horror and stunned disbelief. She looks at Brad and demands, 'Are you cooking poos for dinner, Daddy?!' On first impressions, Rylee did not judge that we were having sausages for dinner.

Young and old, we make judgement calls quickly based just on what we see.

My style personality is what we call in the business (I

just wanted to say that), 'a dramatic feminine'. I'm not going to go into too much detail, but I will give you an example of my dress style. I like to wear heels. Not just heels, but high heels. Not quite Lady Gaga height, but up near that. Heels are feminine. The height makes it dramatic. If I wear a dress, which I like to do, it's feminine. It might be on the shorter side, the more fitted side, in a bold colour, pattern or print — this makes a feminine dress dramatic. (Lesson over.)

I have almost always had long hair — but there was one time I didn't. During that time a judgement call was made. A stone was thrown (probably not intended to hurt, but it did). That shaped me and so I grew my hair long and it hasn't really been short since.

When I was about nine or ten, I had my hair cut off into a short bob style. I remember playing in a park one day and a boy of a similar age came up and asked, 'Are you a boy or a girl? I can't tell.'

Oh, the horror!

I answered incredulously, 'I'm a girl!' Nature has since taken its course and that question wouldn't be asked, but for me at that time and stage in my life, that comment shaped me. My femininity was challenged.

I'm grateful to be comfortable in my own skin now and in how I present myself. It's also a privilege for me to help men and women feel more confident in their outward appearance.

It's not only the outward clothing styles that people struggle with, but their own skin. Some children, teenagers and adults feel as though they have been born into the wrong-gendered body and want to change this. Either through clothes, drugs, surgery, or all of these options. It is so easy to judge, to criticise and sometimes to stare at those who present differently. You might even wonder, 'How could you?' Yet I know, and am still learning, that judging and throwing stones doesn't help anyone.

It's far better to be kind. Be kind and journey with the people who cross your path. Everyone is trying to do life the best they can. So take the time to find out their realities, their backstories, rather than make a harsh judgement call within three to five seconds and then throw hurtful, unhelpful stones.

Stones always leave bruises, some deeper and more damaging than others.

The sinless one among you, go first: throw the stone.

— Jesus

Backstories And Secrets

In my life, I have often been privy, for want of a better word, to people's backstories. I've been able to glimpse behind their tightly-closed, perfect-looking front doors like I talked about in chapter eight. From day one in the police as I started to attend jobs, I realised that so much happens in secret that people don't want others to know. Why? Maintaining pride, I guess, and trying not to experience embarrassment.

I understand that. I didn't want people to know we couldn't have children. I was embarrassed. In my eyes I wasn't 'normal'. No one said that to me; it was my perception. But it was also my reality. Brad and me were actually quite 'normal'. Thousands of couples struggle with fertility issues. But this was still something we kept behind closed doors for a long time.

It was always a humbling and sometimes awkward experience to walk into a situation where police have been called to deal with people's secrets. What had previously been contained has now bubbled over, oozing out from behind their lovely painted doors and over past their manicured lawns into the open for all to see and often to hear. Their secret is out.

Pleasant public perception, versus secretly-hidden realities.

I remember working a late shift when we had to attend a death at a semi-secret gay club. It wasn't widely advertised, but people in the gay community knew of its existence and location.

A man arrives at the club at about 5 pm. He meets another man and they spend some time together in a private room. That's when we get involved. We receive a call at about 6:30 pm from the club to say a fifty-year-old has died on their premises. We arrive and uncover a tragic story. The door is bursting open and secrets are oozing out.

This man is a husband, father and privately gay. No one from his family or close circle of friends knows. He is married, and he and his wife have two young teenage children. He has been living a secret double life for a couple of years.

Today is his fiftieth birthday.

He has gone to the club to meet the man he has been having an affair with, before attending what he thinks is going to be a quiet dinner with his wife. Little does he know she has planned a large surprise party to celebrate his birthday.

While with his friend the man dies from a heart attack.

His friend is obviously distraught when we arrive. He has just lost the person he loves. He manages to fill us in on the secret double life his friend has been living. He is very conscious of and concerned about the trauma and shock that is about to unfold for the man's unsuspecting family and friends.

Checking through the deceased man's property we locate his phone. His friend unlocks it for us and that's when we see the many, many missed calls and texts starting to mount up from his wife: 'You're late.' 'Where are you?' 'Are you okay?' 'Call me, I'm getting worried.'

My partner, sergeant and I stay at the club to deal with all that has to be done. Another unit is dispatched to the restaurant where they find the waiting group of about thirty people. Friends, work mates, family, including his wife, children and elderly parents all eagerly anticipating the man's arrival, waiting to yell 'surprise!' and celebrate his birthday. As the two police officers walk into that restaurant you can only begin to imagine the life-changing surprises that do unfold.

His wife, who had planned the event, receives the most shocking and unbelievable news. Along with everyone else in attendance she has to start working through and processing for herself, and for her children, all that has been revealed.

In this moment I'm face-to-face with raw tragedy — a heartbroken man standing before me, his loved one dead — there must only be the response of kindness and comfort. No judgement at their affair. I bring comfort not because it's my job, but because, like him, I am human. This man needs compassion, not stones. I can be like the Jesus in my bible.

My fellow officers also deliver compassion and comfort that night to the wife, coupled with devastating news.

Where there are secrets, there will be consequences.

Tiger Woods had a secret. It became public to the world when the rear window of his car collided with a golf club wielded by his betrayed and angry wife.

Bill Clinton had a secret. 'I did not have sexual relations with that woman.'

Lance Armstrong, Marion Jones, Nadzeya Ostapchuk and Maria Sharapova, just to name a few, had secrets. Drug tests do not lie.

Josh Duggar had a secret. 2015: The Ashley Madison website, set up to facilitate extramarital affairs. Josh Duggar, along with thousands of others, had his secrets exposed when this online door opened, when the harsh light of day exposed what was being done in secret.

Josh, an American TV personality and a conservative Christian. His secret was out. His parents had nineteen children and a TV show had publicised their lives. Josh was married with four children of his own. But then the light exposed the secrets of Ashley Madison and out oozed his reality. Not only had Josh being using the site, but he was addicted to internet porn, had had affairs and had even sexually abused his sisters.

Josh was reported as saying, 'I have been the biggest hypocrite ever. While espousing faith and family values, I have secretly over the last several years been viewing pornography on the internet and this became a secret addiction and I became unfaithful to my wife. The last few years, while publicly stating I was fighting against immorality in our country I was hiding my own personal failures.'

When I see stories like this flash up on my TV or read about them in the newspaper, I shake my head and a condemning little voice pipes up, 'Be sure your sins will find you out.' It's so hard not to judge, but I'm trying.

Jesus, if he was on earth today, would say: 'You who are without sin, you can cast the first stone.' I would have to put down my stone and walk away.

Jesus? He would look at Tiger, Bill, Lance, Josh and all the others and say, 'What you've done is wrong, but you can be forgiven. There will be consequences, but there is a way out.' *But there must be a penalty for a crime or a wrong committed, otherwise there is no justice, right?* This is how my mind works.

I often think that if you lined us all up, the human race in our birthday suits, we are all pretty much the same. We all enter the world in the same fashion and we all end up breathing a last breath at some point. All the same, just trying to do life the best we can with what's in the middle (another chapter is coming up based around that particular word) probably means keeping secrets from others — who have just as many secrets as ourselves.

Some of us strive so hard to make a good impression. Some of us are always wishing and wanting whatever others have, and therefore never really feel satisfied with what we actually do have. Some of us happy with who we are.

I have been and can be all of the above.

As I've said while sharing my journey so far, everything I have seen, done, heard and experienced has made me the person I am today. Every part of me, inside and out. How I look, behave, dress, act and react. My personality, my habits, good and bad.

I've often worked hard to put on a front that all is well — that I'm calm and in control on the outside — when so many times in the police and through my journey with infertility, this was not the case. There was utter chaos and brokenness behind the scenes. These were secrets I didn't want anyone to know.

Why not? Why didn't I want to let my guard down, so to speak? It was because I was afraid of not being seen as perfect or in control. But none of us is, so why do we try so hard to portray ourselves that way? I think it's because of our backstories. I have been shaped and moulded along my journey, always needing and liking to feel in control. When this gets challenged in any area of my life, I fight. I fight even harder to maintain and portray control.

The journey of infertility pushed my buttons about control and my total lack of it. It also pushed my buttons about injustice. I felt I had been wronged by not being able to make babies in the way everyone else seemed able to. This was not fair and seemed so very unjust. I needed to keep processing these emotions. To make sense of the 'whys?' To understand the point behind the pain — otherwise, what is the point? For me, for my friends, for those I have dealt with, and for all the injustices I see play out on the TV before me.

Also, sadly, for my children when they also suffer loss.

Until one has loved an animal, a part of one's soul
remains unawakened.

— Anatole France

Midnight And Cutie

They were famous by aged three, but by three-and-a-half years of age both had died, within exactly one week of each other. Like a couple that has been married for sixty years, sometimes when one dies, it's like one half of the other has died too. It's too much for the survivor to bear, so somehow they shut down. The will to live has gone, the mind says no more, and the body soon follows.

It was Easter and Father was away. Father was against the idea from the start. Mother had sowed the seed, kept watering it, and then when Father went away, it was time. Time to reap what had been sown.

She calls from a cell phone, 'I've done a check and there are four of them to choose from. There's a sale on. It's a long weekend, perfect timing, what do you think?' He has no choice.

The little one knows the secret. It's hard for her to contain it but she's doing her best. Joy emanates from every part of her little being. She knows the older one will be so happy, unbelievingly so.

School pick-up time, 3 pm. In the car, the little one starts: 'Guess where we are going?' Before any answer can

231

be given, more questions are fired at the older one: 'Guess where? Guess what we are going to do? Guess what Mum has planned? Guess what Dad has said we can do?' Guess, guess, guess!

'Enough!' explodes the older one. 'I hate secrets and surprises — just tell me.'

'We are almost there,' consoles Mum, 'Just another couple of minutes ...'

We enter the store, the older one has a light bulb above her head and it is starting to glow, albeit dimly, cautiously. But it's glowing. Little one has run to the target. 'Oh, this one, I want this one! Please Mum! Look Tayla, look how cute it is! I think I'll call him Cutie, he's sooooooo cute!'

And so our journey as guinea pig owners begins. Just two: two boys, good friends. Two is enough. Cutie for Rylee, and Midnight (picture the colour) for Tayla.

House, food, hay, drinking bottle, toys, bedding sawdust, a list of what to feed and what not to feed ... and a long list of expectations. A booklet like this would have been helpful when bringing babies home from the hospital (just saying), but it seems the sellers of guinea pigs are a more advanced and realise how crucial an instruction booklet can be.

So we head home with full instructions on how to care for our new pets. Well, the girls' new pets. Their responsibility — one hundred per cent theirs, not another thing for Mum to deal with in the mornings! (I know you're hearing me on that one, those of you with pets!)

The hutch is built beautifully by Mum and daughters. Father can't believe the photos of the before pile of building materials and the finished product (amazing what can be achieved when following instructions step by step!), now equipped with two 'live rodents', as he affectionately called them.

Three fun years later, two trips to the vet for injections

for mites (not mentioned in said handbook) and with guinea pigs 'animal sat' by lovely friends, family and neighbours whenever we went on holidays. Many dollars spent on hay, bedding, muesli and fresh vegetables. Many mornings before school in the middle of cold, wet, windy Wellington winter days, proud parents watch as their two young ladies diligently care for their two babies. Fulfilling all the responsibilities needed to care for two wee animals. 'We'll take good care of them; you won't have to do anything.' *You did, girls. Well done!*

Midnight and Cutie had many adventures. Taken to school to be 'lovingly' and 'gently' held by five and seven year olds. Pushed around the driveway on scooters. Gently strapped onto a remote controlled car, which went well till the crash. (Not good.)

Both guinea pigs even experienced an unapproved, unwanted sleepover on their own. Somehow not put back in their cage and not discovered till the next morning. 'How can Cutie, how can Midnight not be in their cage!' No escape routes in sight. Horror, distress, tears .... then relief. Molly the cat seems to be hanging around a pot plant where the guinea pigs had played while their cage was cleaned. Lost was now found. Cold and hungry, but found. (This happened twice, even after stern lectures.)

In 2015 in the *Dominion Post* newspaper there was, every day, a picture of the Pet of the Day. Always cats and dogs. 'Mum, please can we take a photo of Cutie and Midnight and send it in to the paper for Pet of the Day?'

'Okay, I don't know if they'll get in though.'

Animals were suitably dressed in Mr Potato Head outfits. Yellow, round glasses for Midnight and a fabulous green baseball cap for Cutie. Photo taken and sent. Days, weeks passed. No photo in the paper. All forgotten till one morning, staring back at me from the paper, were our dear rodents in all their finery. A special mention made that they had raided the Mr Potato Head dress-up box — and Cutie did bear a huge resemblance to Mr P. in colour and size. The spitting image.

Much rejoicing! More papers had to be purchased for each child to have a copy, taken to school, news shared — *the school must know*. Famous rodents and very proud owners.

Then tragedy struck.

It crept up so quickly, one Friday. Before school: 'Mum, Midnight is not his normal self. He's not eating the same and not moving the same. I think you should take him to the vet today.'

'Well, let's just see how he is after school. We'll see if he's a bit better this afternoon.'

'I'm just saying, Mum, he's not the same. I know, I'm his mum.' Good call.

Same day, 4 pm after school, little one heads out to check on the guinea pigs for bath time. Comes running, 'Mum, I think Midnight's dead!'

'Rylee, are you sure? This is not something to joke about.'

'Truly Mum, he's not moving. Come and see!' Indeed, Midnight, laying how guinea pigs don't. Under his container of hay, still and cold. Very, very cold.

Little one looking into my eyes, hopeful. 'Is he alive, Mum?'

'No love. I'm sorry, he's not. He is dead.'

Automatic tears. 'I have to tell Tayla.'

'Maybe let me tell her, Rylee.'

'No, I'm going to tell her!' She runs into the house into the lounge where Dad and sister are standing. Through tears and sobs: 'Tayla, Midnight's dead.'

In a blink of an eye the brain processes what it has heard, then disbelief, then sadness, then tears. So hard to see two upset daughters going through their first taste of death and loss. Family gathers outside so that all can confirm Midnight's death. Father gets the shovel, children won't touch guinea pig, so Mum does the honours.

To the garden goes the procession and under a lemon tree a grave is dug. Tayla manages to lie Midnight in the ground and puts the first shovel of dirt over him, mixed with tears. Everyone is to say some words, Father included. He does quite well.

The older one doesn't want to tell a soul, while the little one wants to put a death notice in the paper — the school needs to be advised, as do all her friends and classmates.

'No!' yells older sister. 'It's not your guinea pig that's died and I don't want to tell anyone.' Compromise, little one can text best friend, grandparents and uncle, but no discussion in front of Tayla is to be had.

Cutie is cuddled by Rylee, given some freshly picked grass and gently told, 'Midnight is dead, he's gone to Heaven and is happy, but Cutie you are going to be by yourself now.' More tears — yes, from me too.

Saturday, all is well. Sunday, visitors over for lunch are told. Yes, the hutch on the front lawn now contains just one guinea pig. Tayla manages to tell the story, adding, 'I told Mum she should have taken him to the vet, but she didn't.' Noted.

First impression of Cutie, as said by all the visitors who looked at him that Sunday, 'He is the biggest guinea pig I've ever seen! He's huge.'

He was. *Was.*

Monday: 'Mum, Cutie hasn't eaten any of his food.'

'Oh?' Sure enough, it's all still sitting on his plate, untouched. 'I think he will be sad because he's missing Midnight. He'll be okay, just make sure you give him lots of cuddles. You too, Tayla. Remember, you're his auntie and you still need to help Rylee look after Cutie.'

Tuesday morning: 'Mum, there is no poop in the

newspaper (unheard of!) and Cutie still hasn't eaten any of his food.' We file out to have a good look at Cutie and see he has crusty circles around his eyes. Dry tears. It breaks my heart. Cutie is really missing Midnight and it looks like he has been crying. Right, lots of cuddles required. Rylee manages to handfeed him one strip of carrot. Well, that's good.

Wednesday, full food bowl, empty newspaper, no mess. Sad crying eyes. After school on this beautiful sunny evening, Cutie is popped into a warm bath. His eyes are washed and suddenly he starts to preen and clean himself as he usually does, but only for a minute, then he stops. As though, just for a moment his life is normal and he had woken from his bad dream. But then, realisation. His best mate has gone. He sits in the bath, purring happy, yet heartbrokenly sad.

Rylee watching on, 'Mum do you think he'll be okay? He's usually really fat, but he's starting to look at bit smaller? What can we do?'

Dr Google. Sometimes, after the death of a guinea pig, the remaining pet will mourn and possibly go off his food if they have been very close. Maybe try placing a soft cuddly toy in the hutch with the lonely guinea pig? 'Oh, that's perfect, Mum! I'll get my toy Lumpy from Winnie the Pooh. Cutie can snuggle with him.'

As soon as Lumpy is placed in the hutch, Cutie moves faster than we've ever seen him move before and buries himself under Lumpy. Lumpy doesn't respond, obviously.

I'm woken in the night, 1 am glaring on the red alarm clock beside my bed. Cutie on my mind. *Please Jesus, if he's not going to get well, can you help him go really soon; otherwise, please help him get better.*

Thursday, Lumpy is abandoned. Cutie has realised this is not his best mate, but a cruel trick. I spy Father — yes, Father! — going out to the hutch, lifting the lid and patting,

Cutie on the head: 'Come on little guy, you can get better.' This makes me well up.

Thursday night we decide that, come Friday, if still no food is eaten and the hutch is still poo-less, a visit to the vet is on the cards.

Friday morning I wake with a sad sense of dread in my stomach. I just feel it. I head downstairs and see the girls happily eating breakfast. Tayla finishes first and heads out to clean Cutie's cage. 'I'll come with you T,' I say.

The lid is lifted on the hutch. I watch my daughter's face. She looks at me, 'He's dead.'

'Are you sure?'

'I know, Mum. He's dead.'

I check, his eyes closed, peaceful, still framed with a crusty ring of tears. Lumpy, discarded at the other end of the hutch, looks on hopefully.

Rylee comes around the corner, happily singing, but stops when she sees Tayla and me looking at her. 'Rylee, love, I'm really sorry, but ...'

'Cutie's dead.'

'Yes, he is love, I'm really sorry.'

Heartbroken child. Rylee looks in the hutch, 'Do you want to hold him or touch him?'

'No, he's not the same anymore.'

Mum, again, gets to do the honours.

A week to the day, the second funeral is conducted. Father wielding shovel, followed by crying girls and weeping mum, carrying cold, dead guinea pig, with Lumpy bringing up the rear. Cutie is buried on the other side of the lemon tree near his best mate Midnight.

Lumpy, for all the good he did, is also buried with Cutie. Kind words are spoken, even from Father: 'You were so cute.'

Little one can only sob, 'I love you, Cutie!' Snot and tears cover her wee face.

Everyone must be told this time. Text to Nana and Grandad. School friends and teachers are also told. 'Each time I tell someone Mum, it gets easier.' Grief dealt with differently than older sister.

I see Father take his little one in strong arms and whisper, 'I'm so sorry Rylee, it's very sad, isn't it?'

'But you called them rodents, Dad. You didn't really love them!'

'No, but they were your pets, and you loved them. I could see that and so I'm very, very sad for you.'

All part of life. Death. On this earth death is inevitable for all living creatures, big, small, fur covered and not. The Father wants to protect his child, but understands the reality. The Father grieves with the child, because he understands, feels and shares the pain. As his child mourns, so does he.

I would humbly suggest that this is how God — who some call their Heavenly Father — journeys with us. God knows exactly how we are feeling, sees our loneliness, disappointments and heartbreaks. He sees the private tears we cry behind closed doors. God knows all about the secrets we try to contain. He would desperately love to bring comfort, if we'd let him, when a secret becomes too heavy and messy to contain and the oozing process begins.

'Nothing in all creation is hidden from God. Everything is naked and exposed before his eyes, and he is the one to whom we are accountable' (Hebrews 4:13, NLT). Like a good father, God longs to hold us close and comfort us.

'But God is in Heaven,' you say. 'I can't see this God you are talking about!'

That's true. But for me, God's comfort is felt and given in many tangible ways. Remember my double flower delivery? Remember the bible verses, friends' encouragements? Tangible, perfect and timely. Bringing comfort. Remember the money for the lady's ceiling in Suriname? Tangible, perfect and timely.

After I started to talk openly about our IVF journey, and when I was recovering from surgery, friends were with me through my highs and lows. Listening ears and comforting arms to hold me. Thoughtful cards, emails, letters ... and a ukulele. A song, a vista in nature, a poem, words in a book— all tangible ways God has spoken to and met my needs over the years. When like a child, I've called and cried, God like a father, has answered and comforted.

I don't believe God created us to do this life alone. Oh, we try! I've certainly tried. *All my secrets!* But we need to be willing to do life with God and let others in to help.

Here's the best analogy I have for you ...

We have had both our children immunized throughout their young lives. From babies, as toddlers, pre-school, and now school-aged. Understanding what is to come, the Father (yes, in our case, Brad took the girls, every time, to the doctors for their injections — for which I'm so grateful!) holds his most precious gift in his arms as bare, unblemished skin is revealed. The baby or toddler looking totally trustingly into Dad's eyes, wondering what is happening. But no fear, Dad is holding me.

Then ... pain. *Sharp, sudden!* A needle enters that plump, perfect wee leg. Dad doesn't make it stop, he is holding his child tighter, speaking soothing words, but not stopping the pain. *Dad, what are you doing?* Then more pain, another injection. *What is going on?* A lack of understanding, but having to trust while held in her father's arms.

I've held my four-year-old while a doctor 'fixes' her broken arm. 'It hurts Mum. Make her stop!' Tears.

'I know, little one, but the doctor is going to make it better. She just has to move it a bit first. I understand it hurts.' More tears, this time from me. I desperately want my baby to feel no more pain. I don't want her to go through this, but I know it is necessary for her healing. Holding my baby, crying with her, not letting her go as she journeys through the pain, but also not stopping that pain.

The trust of childlike faith. *Do my parents love me and want good for me?* Yes, I believe they do, because they've told me and my journey with them proves this.

God doesn't want me to be childish in my thinking and reactions as I go through life. But what he does ask of me is to have childlike faith and trust in him. Despite all I might see, feel and experience, as a loved child is able to trust themselves to the care of a good parent, so I believe I am — *we are* — able to trust ourselves to the care of our loving God.

As an adult, we know this life we find ourselves living can be unbearably unfair and sad sometimes. Unjust, inhumane and cruel. Cut short too early, too often. I felt injustice as we stood as a family and buried our children's guinea pigs that week. Death can seem unjust even for cute rodents.

I ponder: 'Is it life itself that causes pain and injustice? Is it the people in it, the people doing life around us that are the cause? What about those who seem to get dealt a really bad hand through no fault of their own?'

It simply isn't an adventure worth telling if there aren't any dragons.

— J. R. R. Tolkien

Middle Earthies

I love Mount Maunganui and our family has enjoyed many summer holidays in this idyllic place.

Mount Maunganui is situated on the East Coast of New Zealand's North Island. It has a beautiful coastline of white sand, stunning beaches and the weather is usually perfect. There is also a mountain, funnily enough. 'The Mount', or its official name 'Mauao', meaning 'caught in the light of the day', is two hundred and thirty-two metres high and 3.4 km around the base.

Brad and I are a competitive couple, so most years we chase bragging rights for the one who can run to the top of the mountain first, without stopping or walking. After a while, because we could both manage to run it without stopping, fastest times had to be added into the equation. (Did I mention we are competitive?)

Well, one day — pre-operation — I decided I'd give it a good go to reach the top of The Mount without stopping, focused on that fastest time goal.

My journey starts out beautifully. Hardly anyone else around and the sun hasn't even begun to rise. The journey around the base of the mountain is scenic and peaceful, rich in nature and views of the ever-changing powerful sea. There are a few ups and downs on the track, but nothing too difficult to cope with.

But then I arrive at the part of the mountain where I need to decide whether to head up or go home. *Up or home? Up!* From here it's pretty much all uphill, whether it be running the track or climbing copious amounts of stairs. I know it's going to be hard because I've been to the top before — so I also know how stunning and rewarding it is to get there.

About half-way up I'm still running. Self-encouragement is going on in my head: *You'll have bragging rights if you do this!* I'm sure my heart rate is knocking 200 beats per minute. Stinging sweat drips in my eyes. I can't easily acknowledge the few people I meet on the track. I only have enough strength for myself.

I reach a clearing, and if I'd take a moment to look out amongst the trees, I would see the sun rising. But because of my pain and focus, I don't see it. It's there; I just don't notice.

If I lift my sight I would see that powerful blue ocean stretching into the distance. The vista is beautiful, but it's not for me right now. I'm too busy just staying alive, so focused on pushing through my pain and simply taking that next step. So I don't see the beauty that's all around me.

I know some of you are saying, 'Just stop woman! Are you nuts?' Yes, probably, but it's not in my nature to stop — I'll go till I've nothing left. I can't show weakness. You should understand that about me by now! So I keep moving, the bush closes in around me again and the view is gone.

I finally reach a set of stairs that beats me and I slow to a walk. And that's a secret right there! Because in my mind, this is failure. (Silly, I know.) I notice another couple is in front of me. The guy, who I find out is called Andy, is at the top of the steep stairs, encouraging his female friend.

She has all the right gear for running. She is looking good

on the outside for her journey. Fluro-pink running shoes with branded runner's socks. Fitted lycra pants and top in matching hues. Cap on. Sweat band around wrist. Heart rate monitor attached.

First impressions? Yeah, she looks the part. But second impressions? Despite all the right gear, this journey for her is still very hard and painful — physically and mentally.

Andy is dishing out encouragement for his friend, so I take this on board for myself. (Thank you, Andy!) I make it to the top of the stairs behind the female runner. Andy turns to take off again, much to the disgust of his friend, who breathlessly says, 'Andy, please, just give me a break, won't you!' Andy, bless him, does stop as his friend assumes the hands-on-knees recovery position.

I get my second wind and despite how I'm feeling, I know it's only this one set of stairs that have beaten me and I'm getting close to the top. I also know I can rest there. When I do stop, normal breathing can resume, the pain in my legs will start to ease and the view will be spectacular. I know this, but that doesn't make the last part of the journey any easier.

I arrive at the top of the mountain. I stop, I pause and I rest.

And then I look back to see how far I've come. I don't remember the pain anymore; it is already fading into insignificance. The pain doesn't matter at all to me now. Sure, I wish I'd taken the time to watch the sun rise, but in the midst of my all-consuming drive to survive, my pain was all consuming. But now I take in the awe-inspiring 360-degrees of stunning beauty from the top of the mountain.

The sun has risen and the sea is glistening. I am completely surrounded by beauty of creation. The mountain I've just ascended looks small compared with what I can see. My view has changed.

The destination was worth the journey.

Here comes Andy and friend. They arrive together. Both look pleased, relieved and tired. Their faces also say it was well worth while sticking with the journey.

We smile at each other, an acknowledgement of our 'well done, it was hard but worth it, aye?' solidarity. I feel like running over and hugging them, the comradeship of achieving something tough together. (I don't.) Sometimes a little encouragement does wonders. It really does help to journey through the tough stuff with people focused on the same goal.

I ran to the top of that mountain knowing it would hurt physically for a while, but also knowing what awaited me. I knew that once I reached the top, my view would be completely different and worth every second of my hard journey. I had a hope and a faith in the journey and its outcome. As the bible says: 'Now faith is being sure of what we hope for and certain of what we do not see' (Hebrews 11:1, NIV).

People get tattoos all the time, even though they know it will hurt. In the beginning, they look at the picture of what will ultimately be the end result on their body. But the middle — *the journey* — can be painful. Or so I'm reliably told.

Ears, tongues, noses and other interesting parts of the body are pierced. Despite the pain. People get Botox, face lifts and all sorts of surgery done, all for the end result. That's the goal. A lot of women choose to have more than one baby — the end result is their focus, not the 'during'.

In 2015, Brad and I trained with a friend for about three months to run a marathon. We trained weekly together, encouraging each other through our training sessions. Strong wind and rain made for some hard training runs. Our goal? To finish. And we did. Our second goal? Run it under four hours. We did. Three hours, forty-nine minutes. *So relieved!* But sometimes, in the 'during' of all those hours of running? Man, it was hard and painful!

We are willing to go through pain when we are focused on the end result, the destination. If we can see a purpose for our pain.

When we have an understanding of our goal we are willing to persevere, whatever it takes. It is so much harder to go through pain of any sort when we have no idea of when and how it will be resolved. When we don't know what the end result will be, this makes the journey much harder. *Will all the pain, emotional or physical, be worth it?*

Every good story has a beginning, a middle and an end.

The beginning sets the scene. Characters are introduced, the plot starts to develop and play out.

The beginning: 'In the beginning, there was God.' If you haven't already read it, check out the book of Genesis to read about the creation of the world.

Genesis tells us about God creating a perfect, breathtakingly beautiful, non-pain, non-suffering, non-evil, sinless earth. And then adding some characters: Adam, Eve and animals. The scene is set.

The middle: where the guts of the story takes place. The drama. The deception and deals, the twists and turns. Pain, joy, devastation, disaster, euphoria and elation. Characters are developed. They come and go. Plots thicken. There is injustice. There is death. And so many 'whys'. In our bible story, enter the snake, apple, Eve, Adam, sin. The story gets pretty ugly pretty quickly. Basically, things on earth are never the same again.

The end: you can often tell the end is drawing near when you sense everything is coming to a head. Things are falling into place; you start to see how things might pan out. At the end of a story — *the end of a journey* — our full understanding of what has been going on all along comes to light. All is revealed, the dots are connected, the whys are answered and we go, 'Oh, I get it now!' We needn't have worried, the author knew what was going on and had already written the ending.

From the moment we are born, we gather information and understanding that shapes us along our journey. We want to know the 'whys' of life. (I know I do!) But when it comes to pain, suffering, injustices and the like, the why — making sense of it in this lifetime — is hard to grasp or even start to understand.

In Matthew 24, Jesus says, 'You will hear of wars and threats of wars ... nation will go to war against nation, and kingdom against kingdom. There will be famines and earthquakes in many parts of the world ... Sin will be rampant everywhere, and the love of many will grow cold. But the one who endures to the end will be saved ... see I have warned you about this ahead of time' (NLT). Well, every night on the news I am surely seeing all of this!

Jesus, as usual, just tells it like it is. He doesn't hide the fact that the journey (what I like to call 'the Earthies', or 'Middle Earthies' for those of you from New Zealand), isn't going to be all roses! That's how I see it. And for me, this is how I make sense of things sometimes just too hard to comprehend.

The beginning, before sin: Adam and Eve hanging out naked, blissful gardeners in their perfect garden, happy with free will and life as it was supposed to be. But then, life takes a turn towards the dark side, and sin (with all its symptoms of wrongdoing, injustice, selfishness and greed) enters the world.

'*The middle*', the '*meantime*': That's now. Here on earth, doing life the best we can while evil exists and creation struggles. We live in a beautiful world, yet often because of life's circumstances, we can't see the goodness all around us. And at the same time, our consumer lifestyles are placing a huge toll on our bodies and on our planet.

The end, which can come at any stage for any of us: I guarantee that at some point my heart and yours will stop beating. I know that no matter how good my fitness regime and how many vitamin pills I consume, my wonderful yet decaying body will one day cease to be. I don't want to sound morbid, but however clever and brilliant the world's scientists and doctors, I know my body — in the form it is in now — cannot and will not last forever.

End of story. *Or is it?*

Given that life and death are a guaranteed fact for our entire human race, with no one immune, I would like to think everyone has at least spent some time searching for the answer that satisfies them and brings them peace.

Whether that search ends in the belief that your heart stops and there's nothing more. Or that you come back as something/someone else and life starts all over again. Or that you'll go some other place after death, but you're not sure what that looks like. Or that you believe Jesus, God's son, died for you, so when your heart stops beating, your spirit — that essence of who you are — gets to spend eternity in Heaven. And that Heaven is a place where there is no such thing as pain and suffering, no more judging, no more secrets. No more stones to be thrown.

When my heart stops, I know that's not the end for me. In fact, since I'm being honest, death doesn't worry me in the slightest.

I hope you have a friend who professes to have a relationship with Jesus (and not just someone who says they are 'a Christian', because there can be a huge difference!). I hope you know someone who believes Jesus is the Son of God and that Jesus is their friend. Have a chat to them about this. Ask some questions about the relationship they have with Jesus.

Head along to a church, attend an Alpha Course, grab a copy of the bible and some helpful Christian books on God. For example, *The Case for Christ* (now also a movie) or *The Case for Faith* by one-time atheist and journalist Lee Strobel.

My challenge to you is to make an informed decision on what you believe and why. I hope you can relax into the choice to let Jesus be your friend. Then when your heart beats for the last time, I know you will be happy and at peace with what comes next.

I get pretty passionate about this, but you know how it is when you've found the best bargain, the best product ever? You get excited and want to tell people about it! Well, from where I sit, this *is* the best bargain ever.

For me, 'the end' means when our time here on earth is over, this will be the moment when we will have full understanding and a different perspective 'from the top'. And we'll go, 'Oh, okay, I get it now!' This will be our 'aha' moment.

Because if this journey we call 'life' is only about living out our allotted years and then it's all over, I don't see much of a point. All the relationships built, friends made, loved ones journeyed with — just for the now, then done and gone? I humbly suggest that if that's all there is, life seems like a waste, a dumb ending to a potentially great story.

Surely, if this was the story, no one would buy or read it? Even if it was really cheap to download from Amazon, it's like a story without an ending. *Ripped off!* Or maybe — just maybe — despite the pain and despite not fully understanding the journey at times, there is God.

But a few questions still need to be asked and answered. We do still need to consider the 'but whys'? I saw and dealt with so many of these as a police officer. Bad, terrible and unfair things happening to good, innocent people.

If there is this all-powerful God, why doesn't he come to the party more? Great question! Because sometimes it does feel as if God is like a so-called 'good' but distant father standing in the corner of a room watching his out-of-control teenagers living it up to the fullest. Watching them make dumb decisions with major consequences for themselves and others. Yet God is doing nothing. *But why? How does that work?*

There is a place called 'heaven' where the good here unfinished is completed; and where the stories unwritten and the hopes unfulfilled, are continued. We may laugh together yet.

— J. R. R. Tolkien

26

Pain And Suffering

Some of the pain and suffering I've experienced in my life comes from a path I've chosen, eyes wide open. Whether it be the pain of trying to run up Mount Maunganui or giving birth. I knew it would hurt, but I did it anyway. I've also experienced pain and suffering because of bad decisions I or other people have made.

It's the same for all of us. Bad decisions, dumb ones, both in words and actions. I've already talked a lot about this in relation to things I dealt with as a police officer.

We have free will. People do terrible things to others that result in much unnecessary pain. People make selfish decisions, unholy decisions. We do things that can have terrible results. If we didn't have free will, we might as well be robots. But, in having free will, our decisions and actions can and do have consequences — for us and others.

Let me share three things: a picture I've seen, excerpts from an interview I've read, and paraphrases of a couple of news articles I've come across ...

The picture: I saw a harrowing picture in a newspaper years ago. I cut it out and kept it. The picture was taken in Africa. It's of an infant.

The toddler is dead and alone. Naked, skeletal, yet stomach grossly bloated by starvation. The child is lying curled up, face down on the dusty dirt. The only other thing in the picture is a huge, hopeful and hungry black vulture. It stands a few metres away, biding its time till maybe the photographer leaves. The scene is heartbreakingly sad.

The interview: I've already recommended a couple of books by Lee Strobel, a self-confessed atheist and former investigative journalist who became a Christian. In his book *The Case for Faith*, Lee interviews a man by the name of Charles Templeton. Heard of him? Chuck Templeton? Still not ringing any bells? No, it didn't for me either. How about Billy Graham then? Yeah, possibly heard of that guy.

Billy and Charles started out as evangelists together, telling people about Jesus. Templeton met Graham in 1945 at a Youth for Christ rally. Roommates and constant companions, the friends would alternate in the pulpit as they travelled around preaching. Templeton founded a church that soon overflowed its twelve hundred-seat auditorium.

Templeton had doubts, his faith wavered, questions came that he couldn't find a satisfying answer to, so he decided there could not be a God.

Lee Strobel goes to interview him a couple of years before Templeton dies in 2001. He writes:

Templeton says, 'I suppose you want me to explain how I went from the ministry to agnosticism ...'

Strobel asks, 'Was there one thing in particular that caused you to lose your faith in God?'

He thought for a moment. 'It was a photograph in Life *magazine,' he said finally.*

'Really?' I said. 'A photograph? How so?'

He narrowed his eyes a bit and looked off to the side, as if he were viewing the photo afresh and reliving the moment.

'It was a picture of a black woman in Northern Africa,' he explained.

'They were experiencing a devastating drought. And she was holding her dead baby in her arms and looking up to heaven with the most forlorn expression. I looked at it and I thought, "Is it possible to believe that there is a loving or caring Creator when all this woman needed was rain?"'

As he emphasised the word rain, his bushy grey eyebrows shot up and his arms gestured toward heaven as if beckoning for a response. 'How could a loving God do this to that woman?' he implored as he got more animated, moving to the edge of his chair.

'Who runs the rain? I don't, you don't. He (God) does – or that's what I thought. But when I saw that photograph, I immediately knew it is not possible for this to happen and for there to be a loving God. There was no way. Who else but a fiend could destroy a baby and virtually kill its mother with agony – when all that was needed was rain?'

These are hard questions. I'm not going to pretend there are easy answers.

The news articles:

'Billionaire to Fund Replica of Titanic' (Dominion Post, 2014). A rich Australian is preparing to build a new version of the *Titanic*. He says forty thousand people had expressed interest in tickets for the maiden voyage. The cost to build is estimated at around $500 million. At the time of writing, the latest with *Titanic 2* is the rebuild has not been started.

The billionaire also owns, among other things, one hundred vintage cars, one hundred and fifty racehorses, five private jets, and a large collection of dinosaur fossils. He is quoted as saying, 'I want to spend the money I've got before I die.'

2014. A picture of five US Aircraft carriers: *USS Dwight D. Eisenhower, USS George H.W Bush, USS Enterprise, USS*

Harry S. Truman, and *USS Abraham Lincoln,* all lined up in port at Nava Station Norfolk, Virginia. The aircraft carriers alone in the picture (there were many more ships in the photo), cost about USD$23 billion to build.

The founder of Mindcraft, thirty-six-year-old Markus Persson, who sold his video game to Microsoft for US$2.5 billion and famously outbid Beyoncé and Jay-Z for a Beverly Hills mega-mansion, paying US$70 million. He was quoted in a September 2015 article as saying, 'I've got everything I wanted in life and I've never felt more lonely in this life.'

Lastly, in 2015. 'In anticipation of King Salman bin Abdulazzia of Saudi Arabia staying, the Four Seasons hotel in Georgetown has done some redecorating, literally rolling out the red carpet and turning everything gold. Gold mirrors, gold end tables, gold lamps, even gold hat racks.'

The Executive Director of Food and Development says, 'The world already produces more than one and a half times enough food to feed everyone on the planet.'

And Oxfam says: 'The world produces seventeen per cent more food per person today, than thirty years ago. The problem is many people don't have sufficient land to grow on or income to purchase enough food. The root cause of the problem is inequality.'

The bible has something to say about this: 'The love of money causes all kinds of evil.' 1 Timothy 6:10 (NCV)

Don't get me wrong. I'm not saying being rich and wealthy and being able to enjoy all this life offers is wrong. Wealth is not wrong. Thank God for people who have the funds to help, and do so. Well done to those who have made money and are able to enjoy luxurious lifestyles. Special mention is often made of Microsoft founder Bill Gates — despite giving away so much of his wealth, he remains one of the world's wealthiest people.

What I am talking about is the fact that on this created

earth there is actually enough. Enough of everything for everyone. We, not God, have created a society where money holds the power.

I'm sure the child in that picture, and the mother and baby in the photo that caused Charles Templeton to reconsider his faith didn't want a ticket for a room on *Titanic 2*. They didn't need or want a million-dollar mega-mansion or a gold cup to drink from. Maybe just $10 worth of food would have been sufficient.

And no, we can't make it rain. That comes from nature, and I believe God made that.

So Templeton was right there. But money — and there is plenty of that — sure does buy food, water, medical supplies and shelter. And the ability to sustain all this for everyone.

An unbalanced distribution of wealth.

Mehmet Ciplak. Don't recognise the name? You will as I describe his actions in late 2015.

A tall, lean man with hunched shoulders. He is wearing a green beret, a red, white and black high visibility jacket, dark pants and boots. He has scooped up from the sea and is now carrying gently and tenderly in his arms the body of a three-year-old drowned boy.

A wee boy by the name of Alan Kurdi. Alan is Syrian. Ciplak, a Turkish policeman, is carrying him from the sea that took Alan's life, onto a beach where Alan, his brother, mother and father were hoping to start a new, safe life. Away from terrorists, away from war, away from where people with free will do inhumane things to other people. Only the father survived the family's quest for freedom. This picture went viral, highlighting the desperation of normal families desperately wanting to escape the horrors of war.

Alan's father, Abdullah, left his home hoping for a safe future with his family in Europe. He returned to Syria, in his words, 'with nothing'.

Constant fighting in the Middle East causes families to flee their country. Families simply wanting to enjoy and live life. But peoples' actions affect others. Selfishness, greed and hate affect others. We all have free will. We all have choices. For better or worse.

As I looked at these pictures and others like them, of poverty and an unfair, unbalanced and selfish distribution of wealth, my heart breaks. I'm upset at the injustice and heartache of the starving, hurting and war-ravaged people of our planet. *This is not fair!*

But what also comes to my mind is that I believe God's heart breaks too — because these people are his children. God's creation is hurting. I just see a photo, but God knows these faces as his own family. He knows their pain and suffering far more than I do and he weeps too.

God didn't need to make us so he could feel complete. We were created so God could love us, and so we, in turn, could love God. Humans don't 'need' to make babies to 'feel completed' — love is the reason and a baby is the most wonderful result. This is the beauty that can come from relationships when they are pure and good.

I want my precious girls, whom I had a hand in creating, to love me because I'm their mum. Not because I can tell them to or force them to, but because they want to. I want their love to be born from relationship. I love my girls unconditionally. I don't love them more when they do well at school or in a competition. Sure, I celebrate with them, but I love them because of who they are, not what they do.

To *make* someone love you isn't love. But love given freely? Well, that's the ultimate blessing of free will.

But, as I said, free will comes at a price.

We ought to give thanks for all fortune: if it is good, because it is good, if bad because it works in us patience, humility and the contempt of this world and the hope of our eternal country.

— C. S. Lewis

27

Darker But Normal

Why God?

Why do children die of cancers and disease? Seriously, what is the point of that?! Why do some people get cancer and survive, when others die? Why does someone live with a crippling disease even though they are the nicest, best person ever, yet the person down the road who does despicable things to children is physically pain free? (I know you'll have your own questions.)

I knew a Wellington police officer by the name of Dean Gifford. He was once nominated for Wellingtonian of the Year. Not just for his work in the police, but also because of the selfless work he'd done raising money for kids with cancer and also for his work to improve the lives of children in the Solomon Islands. Dean died in 2012 after losing his battle with brain cancer. He was forty-one, and left behind a wife and two young children.

Why? What was the point of that? Help me make sense of this, God! For me, the only way I can even begin to make some sense of it is by looking in my bible.

There is a story about a man named Job. I'm grateful his story is in the bible. (If you haven't read it, take a look sometime. It's in the Old Testament. Job has a whole book named after him.)

Basically, Job was a good man. Also very rich — he'd be on the Forbes Rich List today. Blessed with a large family (really important back then). The bible says he was the greatest man around. Selfless, doing good for others and his family.

But then stuff happens for Job. Life goes one hundred per cent pear-shaped.

He literally loses everything: his wealth, his animals and all his possessions. His family and children die. Then his health takes a turn for the worse and he becomes sick. Really sick. All that could go wrong, did go wrong. And now Job had nothing. Nothing but terrible physical, emotional and mental anguish.

His friends start putting up the call: what have you done wrong to be punished like this?

And this is important to note. Job had done nothing wrong. Absolutely nothing. He lived a perfectly good life. And this is where it gets really hard ... as human beings we have a strong sense of justice about this. Good things should happen to good people. And the bad? Well, they should get what they deserve.

So Job was a good man. Minding his own business, like most of us are. Like the Dean Giffords of this world.

Then the phone call comes. And there I am, the police officer knocking at your door, the accident that takes away your ability to live life as you once did. Life has dealt a terrible blow —through no fault of your own.

In the final chapters of the book of Job, God speaks directly to Job.

Job hasn't turned away from God, hasn't stopped believing in God, despite all that has happened. But that doesn't mean he's happy. Quite rightly, he's yelling and crying out to God:

'Why me, why my family, why my health? Why?! What have I done? It's so unfair!'

Just because terrible things are happening that Job doesn't understand the 'why' of, doesn't make him say, 'Oh, that means there is no God.' No, Job still questions.

And here's the key moment — the turning point. It's still hard; God doesn't give answers to Job. Nope. God asks questions, chapter after chapter of questions. You can read the whole thing for yourself, but here's an example:

'Can you shout an order to the clouds and cover yourself with a flood of water? Can you send lightning bolts on their way? Job, are you the one who gives the horse its strength or put a flowing mane on its neck? Have you gone to where the sea begins? Tell me, what were the earth's foundations set on?' God goes on and on.

Some notes in my bible say: 'Is God angry with Job? No. Firm? Yes. Direct? Yes. Clear and convincing? Absolutely. But angry? No. God owes no one anything, no reasons, no explanations. Nothing, because often, if he gave us answers, we couldn't understand them.'

Four-year-old Rylee once asked, 'What do those red and green numbers on the TV mean?' The stock market trading figures and exchange rates had come on the news. Brad and I tried to explain what they meant, using all sorts of analogies — but she just did not get it and told us so.

We knew there was no point in keeping the discussion going, as no matter how we packaged the answer, her four-year-old brain did not get it. She didn't yet have the ability to understand.

Another question, this time from six-year-old Tayla: 'Why can't I watch that programme?'

'Because you will have nightmares.'

'No I won't.'

'Yes, you will.'

I have a smart phone (really, it is!). It stuns me that the girls and I can be sitting having breakfast in our home in Wellington, New Zealand, and we can Facetime Brad when he is in another part of the world for work. Within a matter of seconds there he is, large as life, looking at us. He sees what we can see and then he shows us around his hotel room with his phone.

Do I get the technology behind that? I can't grasp it for a minute!

As I've said, there are still lots of questions I don't know the answers for. This often frustrates my eldest (now tweenaged) daughter. 'You should know Mum, you've been to school!'

I marvel at the 'whys' of how the earth is the perfect distance from the sun so we don't get fried, yet we benefit from its heat. The planet where we just happen to live has gravity, but the moon doesn't. Sir David Attenborough so brilliantly describes how things in nature just 'happen' to work together to complement each other perfectly so species can survive.

If there was a Big Bang when the earth was created and life began because just the right gasses connected at just the right moment in just the right amounts, that's great! But who created these gasses in the first place? Something can't just come from nothing.

Just because I can't understand something — or, for that matter, don't believe in something — doesn't make that thing real or not. It either is or it isn't. It works or it doesn't. It's real or it's not. My understanding of something makes absolutely no difference to its reality.

I don't know why terribly unfair things happen. Why children die before their parents. Why life doesn't turn out as we planned it. Why all the unanswerably heartbreaking things happen. Why my 'but whys' aren't always answered, or at least not to my satisfaction.

But what I do believe is this: I have a finite mind; God is infinite. I (we) ask questions expecting answers. We want answers that make sense *now*. But we are living in that 'Middle Earthies' period. God, who (as I've said) I see as my Heavenly Father, knows my finite mind could not comprehend the answers he could give me. As clever as I am, a lot of the time I simply cannot comprehend the infinite wisdom and mind of the creator God.

I believe God says to us, 'Some things at certain times you won't get. I won't be able to answer your heartbroken cries and questions — not because I can't, but because I'm your father, you're my child and (as it says in Isaiah 55:8, NIV): 'As the heavens are higher than the earth, so my ways are higher than your ways and my thoughts than your thoughts.'

It comes down to the analogy of a parent/adult with child. Adult knowing best, seeing more than the child, seeing the bigger picture, seeing the end result. So we parents say, 'Trust me, I know best.'

In other words: 'Have faith in me as your parent. You can throw a tantrum if you like. You can say, "I don't love you anymore!", slam the door, call me names, turn your back and run away, stop believing in me — it won't change the fact that I'm real and that I will always love you.'

And, like any good parent, our Heavenly Father, waits, arms always open. Which means, for me, God is the only one who will ultimately make sense of the pain and suffering I see, hear about and feel. The injustices I've seen and dealt with.

The end will make up for the sometimes chaotic middle.

In the Bible, Jesus says (in Matthew 18): 'You must become *like little children* to enter God's kingdom.' He didn't say *become children*, with the idea that we just amble along in life not questioning, growing or learning. Jesus said become *like* a child, trusting and growing in our relationship. So I choose to do this.

When Rylee was in hospital getting her broken arm mended, I didn't say, 'I'll just be in the waiting room having a coffee, see you when you've got through the pain stuff.' No, I stayed — as any good parent would. I held her other hand and whispered to her, 'It will be okay, I'm here.'

I cried when she did. Did it take the pain away? No, she still had to go through that, but not alone.

This is why I believe God sent Jesus his son, to teach us it is possible to live on this earth even with all its chaos. In this Middle Earthie-time, God wants to help us.

Jesus came, born of the virgin Mary, and grew from a baby through childhood to adulthood. You still may be in the mindset of: Jesus, he's a good man, a guy written about in a historical book, a hippy of his time, maybe even a prophet. And that's totally fine. But let me tell you though what I believe about Jesus.

Jesus suffered much throughout his life. The night Jesus goes to a quiet place in Jerusalem's Garden of Gethsemane to pray, knowing he will soon be arrested and put to death, he asks his closest friends to come with him. Jesus needs help and encouragement from his friends because he's struggling. It's normal to ask for help. But on this night, they fall asleep. (Friends do let us down sometimes — just as we let them down sometimes. Jesus had normal friends, friends like our friends. Friends like us.)

Jesus, in his deepest time of need, sees his mates sleeping while he's been praying. He feels rejected. He's been let down; disappointed by those he expects the most of. (Just as we get let down and feel pain sometimes — a normal human experience.)

As he's praying, Jesus is talking to his Heavenly Father:

'Dad, please, if it's at all possible, I really don't want to go through this. Please, if there is any other way!'

Luke 22:44 (NCV) tells us: 'Being full of pain, Jesus prayed even harder, sweat was like drops of blood falling to the ground.' But — and here is the child surrendering to the parent he knows, loves and trusts — 'Do what *you* want, Father, not what *I* want.' Despite being overwhelmed by pain and not being able to see the top of the mountain, Jesus says: 'Right now this seems beyond me, but I trust you, I have faith in you.'

Then I read about the physical suffering of Jesus on the cross, the excruciating pain of crucifixion. And again Jesus calls to his father (in Matthew 27:46): 'My God, my God ... Father, Dad ... why have you abandoned me? Why?!' It's normal not to welcome pain or suffering. And it's also normal to question in those times.

In this moment, life is too hard even for Jesus to see the big picture. He is so consumed with the physical, tortured pain of being held to a cross by nails hammered through his hands and feet that he is yelling, 'Why?!' Feeling utterly rejected and abandoned by a father whom he has trusted, loved and talked to daily, Jesus cannot see the big picture. Unbearable, unfair, his life too full of unwarranted pain and suffering. And with his 'why?' unanswered.

So, when I struggle and don't get it and question God (and sometimes these are anger-fuelled questions, just let me say!), thankfully I know I'm quite normal.

Am I (are we) expected to go through life laughing at pain and suffering either simply because we believe in God, or because we mistakenly believe we shouldn't question, wonder or cry out for an explanation? No! Jesus didn't. And if it's good enough for the Son of God to question, it's good enough for you and me.

But most importantly, we are never to give up talking

with God. Praying. Communing. Praying for healing, praying for our families, children, loved ones, for every circumstance we find ourselves in.

Jesus spoke daily with his father. Sometimes his prayers were answered; sometimes, painfully, they were not. But Jesus trusted his Father's heart.

Matthew 5:4 (NIV) says, 'Blessed are those who mourn for they will be comforted.' Unfortunately, it doesn't say, 'Blessed are those who mourn for they will receive an explanation.' Bad things do happen to good people for reasons that are quite beyond us and our finite minds.

In times of crisis, pain and when I see injustices, I have a choice. My choice is to turn my back on God in anger and disbelief and say, 'Because of what I see or experience, you must be either bad or not real.' Or I can say, 'Despite all that is going on in my life right now, despite what I see good people going through, despite the injustices I see, I believe that you, God, are in control and you have a plan.'

I can say, 'I believe that you are good, God, and that you will bring justice where it is so desperately needed. I believe that you, God, love me more than I can comprehend. So I choose to surrender as a child to a parent and trust you, instead of demanding an explanation.

Author Max Lucado, in his book *And the Angels were Silent*, writes:

Lastly, Jesus gives us assurance of completion: 'then the end will come.'

1 Thessalonians 4:16 (NCV) says, 'The Lord himself will come down from heaven with a loud command'. Have you ever wondered what that command will be? It will be the inaugural word of heaven. It will be the first audible message most have heard from God.

'It will be the word that closes one age and opens a new one.

(In other words, finishing the Middle Earthies and ushering in that 'aha' moment.)

I think I know what the command will be. I could very well be wrong, but I think the command which puts an end to the pains of the earth and initiates the joys of heaven will be two words: 'No more.' The King of kings will raise his pierced hand and proclaim: 'No more.' The angels will stand and the Father will speak: 'No more.'

Every person who lives and who ever lived will turn toward the sky and hear God announce: 'No more.' No more loneliness. No more tears. No more death. No more sadness. No more crying. No more pain. No more 'whys'.

God is God, he knows what he's doing. When you can't trace his hand, trust his heart.

I can't wait for the time of 'no more'!

I'm a little pencil in the hand of a writing God, who is sending a love letter to the world.

— Mother Teresa

Not The Ending

In 1992, the Olympic Games were held in Barcelona and a British athlete named Derek Redmond was considered likely to win a medal in the 400m track event.

Reading about Redmond, I discovered he'd missed the 1986 Commonwealth Games because of a hamstring injury. In 1988, at the Seoul Olympics, he had to withdraw minutes before his first heat, having failed to fully recover from tendonitis.

In 1992, the world witnessed a man continually brought down by injuries, who came close to giving up sport altogether, but then trained hard and lined up to again compete at the highest level.

First heat, hope was rising. Redmond ran his quickest 400m in four years. He was feeling good, one hundred per cent. 'I'd had two really good rounds without even trying,' he said.

Semi-finals. Redmond's father, Jim, who is also his coach, is watching from the grandstand with thousands of other spectators. Millions are watching all around the world.

What unfolded was gut-wrenching, heartbreaking and so terribly unfair.

Redmond, off to a really good start. Again, in his words, 'This was unusual for me. I think I was the first to react to the pistol. By the time I'd got upright, I was almost round the bend, much further than usual. I decided to save my energy in case I had to fight for the line.'

But about three strides later Redmond felt a pop. His hamstring had gone. He collapsed to the floor, clutching his leg in pain.

Red Cross workers approached him as Redmond pushed himself back to his feet. He later shared his thoughts from those moments: 'There's no way I'm going to be stretchered out of the Olympics. I also really, really believed I could still qualify. I was hobbling, but I thought I was running. I thought, "If I can only just overtake four people I can still qualify for the final." 'It's not until Redmond looked back on the footage that he realised how slowly he was limping. He was still so focused on the goal.

Then the scene that, no matter how many times I watch it, always makes me cry. From the stands, Jim starts making his way to the track. He pushes track officials out of the way to reach his struggling son.

'I told Derek to stop in case the injury might heal in time for him to compete in the relay,' Jim said.

His son refused.

'Well then,' Jim said, 'we're going to finish this together.'

And they do. Slowly, and with Redmond's pain and grief becoming more and more clear, father and son cross the finish line together.

What made this moment so special was that it brought into focus not just the near-heroic desperation of a single professional athlete, desperate for his goal, but a far more universal theme: the nature of parenthood.

No way would a father give up on his son! When his son

was at his most anguished, the father was there. No words, just actions.

Two years after the Barcelona Games, following an eleventh operation on his Achilles tendon, Redmond's athletic career was over. But he wasn't finishing alone. Redmond had his father by his side and millions of people willing him on. Perhaps unsurprisingly, his courage that day saw him go on to launch second career as a motivational speaker.

Redmond later said, 'Everything I had worked for was finished. I hated everybody. I hated the world. I hated hamstrings. I hated it all. I felt so bitter that I was injured again. I told myself I had to finish. I kept hopping round. Then, with 100 metres to go, I felt a hand on my shoulder. It was my old man.'

And Jim added, 'I'm the proudest father alive, I'm prouder of him than I would have been if he had won the gold medal. It took a lot of guts for him to do what he did.'

Redmond received many messages from his fellow competitors, including this one from a Canadian he had never met: 'Long after the names of the medallists have faded from our minds, you will be remembered for having finished. For having tried so hard, for having a father to demonstrate the strength of his love for his son. I thank you, and I will always remember your race and I will always remember you — the purest, most courageous example of grit and determination I have seen.'

I trust God's promise that he is with me constantly. Not watching from the stands, but on the track with me.

We all need grit and determination to get through life's many 'hamstring' moments. Times and seasons full of grief. Tunnels that seem so dark you don't believe there could be an end to them. What I would offer is that despite the journey, it's actually about how we finish. And for me, the key to this lies in investigating the possibility that there is a Father in

Heaven who is with us. Who will be involved as much or as little as we like. Our choice.

When our bodies fail us, when unfair things happen, when people we trusted and believed in let us down or betray us, God is there. Arm around us, helping us up if we will let him. *Our choice.* But we don't have to do or finish this journey alone.

Wednesday, 16th December 2015, two-and-a-half years after astronaut Tim Peake began training for the International Space Station, with two other crew members. Britain's first astronaut at the station and only its second in space.

Peake's proud and humbled parents were at his launch. Also saying goodbye for six months was Peake's wife Rebecca and their two sons, six-year-old Thomas and four-year-old Oliver. All excited for son, husband and father going off on his mission, but also nervous and sad. There is always risk — always the unknown.

Sitting on the shoulders of his grandfather, little Oliver was heard to cry loudly, 'I want to go with Daddy!' This represents how I feel about my future. I'm an adult and, I would like to think, a reasonably intelligent one. I know a lot of stuff. But there's a lot I don't understand too.

I've probably lived about half my life right now and hopefully have another forty or even fifty years to go. But at some point my heart will stop. That's one thing I can guarantee, one thing I do know. And then, I believe, I will live for eternity with God in Heaven.

I don't know how I'm going to get to Heaven. Literally, that is. I don't have it all figured out in my head what each step will look like when my heart eventually stops beating. I've no idea.

But what I do know is that I trust my Heavenly Father. God says he's prepared a wonderful place for me where there is no more pain, sorrow or terrible things happening to good people. No more injustice. A place where I will be happy and at peace for eternity, hanging out with my family and friends. A place where the Marys and the Alans can also live if they choose to.

When four-year-old Oliver says, 'I want to go with Daddy', he doesn't understand all the technicalities of how that might happen. All he knows is that he is safe when he's with his dad. His dad loves him, has good plans for him and guides him in his life's journey. *So, if Dad's going to space in a big rocket, I want to go too!*

Me too. I'm doing my journey on earth, running my race the best I can. But I know, for a fact, this journey will come to an end. And then ... 'I want to go with Daddy.' I want to go home to my Heavenly Father.

But for now, I'd love to think I have many more chapters of my life here on earth to write about. (Like the *Star Wars* movie franchise that just keeps on giving.) The continuing battle between the good and the dark side is strong. Losses on both sides. Grief, pain and disappointments, along with laughter, love, wins and happy memories.

I want to live each day the best I can, hoping I will wake tomorrow and get to enjoy another day, maybe putting into place lessons from the day before.

At the moment, we're facing the tween years with our children. ('Good luck with that, I hear some of you say. Just wait till they are teenagers and you have two hormonal daughters under one roof!)

I sometimes wonder what my children will decide to do with their lives when their decisions no longer involve me. Jobs, travel, relationships, children? I do need to stop worrying about those 'what ifs' when they sneak in. As I know, amongst the joy, fun and adventure there will also be pain, heartbreak and disappointments. And no parent ever wants to see their child suffer.

I remember so clearly the day I lost one of my precious girls. Me, my eight-month-old and two-and-a-half-year-old ventured to the mall for an outing on a wet miserable day, along with (it seemed) all the other mums and children who lived in our city. (Yes, I'm exaggerating, but you get the point. The mall was very busy.)

We struggle yet manage to find a car park in the parking building. Baby safely secured into the buggy. Toddler standing on the cool three-wheel, skateboard-type attachment at the back of the buggy. Said buggy loaded up with everything needed by a mum with two wee children, and off we go.

We navigate our way around the mall, enjoying a fun time. There are rides to try out, food to eat, toy shops to explore. Then, in the last shop of the day, major stress. Heart dropping in the pit of my stomach disaster.

The large children's clothing shop is child friendly. There's a TV playing cartoons and a small drawing table set up with pens and paper.

Toddler is happily seated in front of the TV and starts colouring in a picture of a butterfly. 'Now, you stay here. Mummy is just going to look at some new clothes for you and I will be back very soon. I'm not going to leave this shop, okay?'

'Okay Mummy.'

I set off manoeuvring the buggy in and out of the many clothing racks and people. Within two to three minutes I decide there's nothing suitable and baby is starting to loudly announce she's hungry, tired and wants to leave.

I return to the drawing table to see the half-coloured picture of the butterfly lying discarded on the table. The TV is still playing, but my child is gone. My head swivels and I start calling her name, not too loudly to start with, but the longer I don't see her wee blonde head appear, the louder my voice gets.

I don't like to make a scene, but in this moment a scene is required.

'Has anyone seen my daughter Tayla? She's two-and-a-half, she has blonde hair, she's wearing ....' I start announcing all this information to no one in particular, but I'm using the voice of a mother who cannot find her child and is starting to worry, quite a lot, so people are looking at me.

My daughter's not in the store. My baby in the buggy is still crying. I want to start doing the same, but I need to keep it together and find my toddler. By now the shop assistants are looking around, calling her name and asking me for more details about her.

I need to go and look for her, so I start to head out of the shop, but then I think what if she comes back and I'm not here? Then I hear, 'Sheryn?' It's a police officer I used to work with. I quickly explain what has happened.

'Okay', he says, 'I'll stay here with your baby and buggy and keep an eye out. You go look for your other daughter.'

'Thank you, thank you!' I say as I rush outside the shop and stop. I look around the mall, which is heaving with people.

It's in this moment my heart completely sinks and the tears threaten to well in my eyes. *I don't know where my baby girl is!* There are masses of people. I don't know which way to turn. I can't see her. All I can see is mums and their children, and I've lost mine.

The 'what ifs' start creeping into my mind, all the worst-case scenarios. *Has someone taken her? Have they got her to a car already?* More and more questions are starting to take over my brain. I whisper a 'please God, help me find her' prayer under my breath. I decide to turn left and walk/run back to the car park.

Again, I get over not wanting to make a scene and start calling my daughter's name. I've got a loud voice when I need it, so I quickly attract attention. People are slowing to look at this mother who is obviously in distress. Everything around me seems to be in slow motion. I'm staring intently at every person, every child, as I process in my mind what my daughter is wearing. I am willing my eyes to find her.

I'm now about twenty metres from the shop, still calling my child's name. Then I see her. I see her back. Her long blonde hair. The familiar clothes I dressed her in that morning. She stands out because she's so little and looks so alone. I call her name again and she turns to me.

My tears leak out with relief and thanks. I see her distraught face mimicking mine, with her own tears of relief.

'Mummy!' she screams. And, yes, just like in the movies we do run to each other. I know people have stopped and are watching, but I don't care. I only have eyes for my baby.

I gather her into my arms as I kneel on the cold hard floor and hold my precious girl as she sobs into my shoulder. She is trying to say something. 'What is it sweetheart?'

'Too tight, Mummy, too tight. I can't breathe.'

'Oh, sorry love!'

As I carry my girl back to the store I see kindly faces smiling at the reunion they have just witnessed. Somehow my ex-work colleague has managed to get my baby to stop crying and he smiles as I walk back into the shop. Again, I say thank you, but it doesn't seem nearly enough.

When we get back to the car and have both calmed down a little, no harsh words are spoken. Too much relief. Yes, there are discussions about doing as Mummy asks, not leaving a store, and reassurance that Mummy would never ever leave you.

'Why did you leave the shop?' I ask.

'I couldn't see you.'

'But I said I would be in the shop and I wouldn't leave you.'

'Yes, Mummy. But I couldn't see you, so I thought you had left me.'

She was trying to find me by going back to where she thought the car was. She couldn't see me or feel my presence, so she thought I had left her behind. Abandoned her.

Sometimes, just like my toddler, when I can't see something or feel or understand it, my perception is my reality. In my daughter's mind, Mum had left the building. And I can see how people might think the same of God. *He can't be real because I can't see or feel him. He can't be real because terrible things happen to good people.*

At this point in my life, I cannot see God. Do I sometimes wish I could? Of course! Yes, like my child, sometimes I've questioned, 'Where are you?'

On those days when I need God to be on the track with me, when I feel like I'm sitting on someone's shoulders watching the rocket blast away, and when I feel like he's left me in the shop by myself, I choose to trust. I look back on God's faithfulness — and I trust.

So, life wide open, when I look back over all I've seen and done, I've felt pain, heartbreak and disappointments. Am I okay? I like to think so.

Did I learn along the way, become stronger in myself and in my faith, become more useful to others because of the trials I've faced along the way? Yes, of course!

As I've said, everything I've been through has shaped me, and I sit here today so very grateful for my life. For every part of it.

I look at my marriage. Brad and I have certainly tested some of those heartfelt marriage vows we so lovingly exchanged over two decades ago! But I love this man with all my heart. I love that we have journeyed together through good and bad. I'm grateful for the experiences we have gone through. For the children we have created. It just takes my breath away.

Are our lives perfect? Of course not. I'm not perfect, far from it — and neither is Brad. But we are a team, and we are committed to doing this journey together and working through our differences. And there are a few! I picture Brad giving a speech at his daughters' twenty-first birthdays. I imagine him walking our girls down the aisle if they decide to marry (not happening till they're both aged around forty, as we've explained to them both!). Becoming grandparents — or again, maybe not. Experiencing retirement, whatever that may look like.

These days, the face and body I see in the mirror in the morning are somewhat different than they used to be. Truthfully, sometimes this is hard for me to accept. But I focus on embracing the fact that I have changed because I have lived, and lived to the full. For this I am grateful.

My body has carried and produced two stunningly beautiful, intelligent, funny and amazingly grounded good children. Laughter is permanently etched around my eyes now. Stress shows in lines on my forehead and has affected my insides drastically. I had twelve fantastic years doing an adrenaline-filled job that I loved with a passion. It took its toll in many ways, but I have no regrets. Again, I am grateful.

My lifelong reality is that God has been so very faithful. I see a purpose in how my life has unfolded. I could not have planned it any better. And after four-plus decades, I have no reason to start doubting God now.

Some 'whys' have been answered. Some 'whys' most definitely have not. But even those unanswered questions do not change the fact that God, who has always been, who is and who will come again, is real. He is good. He is perfect love. He has a plan for me that is full of hope.

And he has a plan for you.

Our stories and journeys will look different, but I believe our last chapter, the one called 'Eternity', can be the same and that it will make all our past chapters pale into insignificance. That stuff we used to worry about? The pain, the loss, the stresses and worries, the 'what ifs'? No more. No more feeling alone in the shop.

Remember wise King Solomon? He once said, 'It is a wonderful thing to be alive! If a person lives to be very old, let him rejoice in every day of life, but let him also remember that eternity is far longer, and that everything down here is futile in comparison' (Ecclesiastes 11:7, TLB).

It is a wonderful thing to be alive and enjoy what every day holds. And as I play my journey forward I picture myself at 'home', sitting in my favourite chair, smiling with my wizened face, rejoicing in all the life going on around me. 'Home' being where I am perfectly relaxed. Not judged, but loved. Comfortably vulnerable in my own skin and at peace.

Yet, as I quietly contemplate this picture of my earthly home and the overwhelming sense of joy and peace that I will feel, I know it is fleeting. This is my story so far, but I know the Greatest Author has already written me into eternity.

Afterword

Honour and enjoy your Creator while you're still young,
Before the years take their toll and your vigour wanes,
Before your vision dims and the world blurs,
And the winter years keep you close to the fire...

... Life, lovely while it lasts, is soon over.
Life as we know it, precious and beautiful, ends.
The body is put back in the same ground it came from.
The spirit returns to God, who first breathed it ...
          Ecclesiastes 12:1-2 & 6-7 (MSG)

Printed in the United States
By Bookmasters